True Colors: Evanston Through Our Eyes

True Colors

Evanston Through Our Eyes

Senior Studies
2017

Shorefront Press
Evanston, Illinois

Shorefront Press
www.shorefrontlegacy.org

Printed in the United States of America

Library of Congress Cataloging-in-Publication Data

Names: Evanston Township High School (Evanston, Ill.)
Title: True colors : Evanston through our eyes / Senior Studies 2017.
Description: First edition. | Evanston, Illinois : Shorefront Press, 2017.
Identifiers: LCCN 2017022350 | ISBN 9781946717009 (paperback)
Subjects: LCSH: Evanston (Ill.) —Race relations—Anecdotes. | Evanston (Ill.) —Social conditions—Anecdotes. | Racism—Illinois—Evanston—Anecdotes. | Discrimination—Illinois—Evanston—Anecdotes. | Community life—Illinois—Evanston—Anecdotes. | Minority high school students—Illinois—Evanston—Biography—Anecdotes. | High school students—Illinois—Evanston—Biography—Anecdotes. | Evanston Township High School (Evanston, Ill.)—Students—Biography—Anecdotes. | Evanston (Ill.)—Biography—Anecdotes. | Oral history—Illinois—Evanston.
Classification: LCC F549.E8 T78 2017 | DDC 305.8009773/1—dc23
LC record available at https://lccn.loc.gov/2017022350

INSTITUTE of **Museum**and**Library** SERVICES

DRIEHAUS FOUNDATION

This project was made possible in part by the Institute of Museum and Library Services #MH-00-16-0024-16

Supported by The MacArthur Funds for Arts and Culture at The Richard H. Driehaus Foundation

Made possible in part by a generous donation from Col. (IL) Jennifer N. Pritzker and Stone Heritage Properties

To Mr. Allen, Mr. Newman and Ms. Walker

Table **of Contents**

Introduction

by Shama Kipfer-Tessler

When beginning this process, I knew I wanted to organize a way to shed light on Evanston's vast inequalities. Inspired by the format of *Hinky Dinks, Sundaes and Blind Pigs*, oral history seemed the most fitting means to share this story, as they tell history through the lens of each individual's experience, which to me is a more transparent form of history. Within my Senior Studies class, my peers shared a myriad of eye-opening stories throughout the first few months of the course, and wanting to share some of these experiences, I began compiling interviews with various classmates.

When interviewing my peers, I tried to remove myself as much as possible within each conversation. With the help of Dino Robinson and Toly Walker I was able to develop several broad questions to prompt each individual. Each interview would begin with, "*Tell me where your parents were born, and why they chose to live in Evanston.*" which was followed by a series of open-ended questions regarding their experience within ETHS, Evanston and District 65. The final questions were, "*Have you seen or experienced prejudice in Evanston and if you're comfortable can you speak to that?*" and "*What change would you like to see within Evanston?*" While the interview questions weren't specifically on the topic of race, the piece as a whole speaks to racial disparities in Evanston, and the inclusion of white people in this book was intentional as their narratives display vast privilege disparities.

The process itself was tedious— as each interview was transcribed word for word. Each of the interviews was anywhere between 10 to 30 minutes. When transcribing I completely removed myself from the transcription, creating a singular dialogue from each individual. The thought behind each portrait was for the reader to be able to both see who's speaking and feel as though they are in conversation with each individual.

One cannot overlook the role my own whiteness played within each conversation and how it could have affected the responses within each interview. White females were by far the most responsive group to show interest in this project, the demographic became so large that I eventually had to cap it at 10 individuals, as the demographic was becoming overpowering in the piece's overall narrative. This responsiveness can easily be tied to my own advertising methods inherently catering towards this specific demographic.

While the intention of this piece is to speak to Evanston's racial disparities, this book preserving the experiences of the Senior Studies Class of 2017 quickly became intersectional, speaking to transphobia, anti-Semitism, xenophobia, sexism and much more that my peers have endured within the community.

The questions evolved throughout the interview process and with each classmate's recommendation. Each interviewee filled out a release form and organized getting their portrait taken on their own time. The title of book itself was workshopped by several members of the class (Laura Tataille, Jameson Ogunbola, Lauren Davis, Shirine Marzouki, Stuart McKean and Oliver Kamholtz-Roberts). Students involved promoted the project to the rest of the class through social media and word of mouth. Maya Madjar helped transcribe many of the interviews, and several classmates proofread and edited the transcriptions. To take credit for this piece wouldn't be fitting as it was a class effort, all I did was compile the interviews, and Dino Robinson, of Shorefront Legacy Center did the rest!

True Colors: Evanston Through Our Eyes

Zack **Begly**

So my mom was born in Port-au-Prince, Haiti and my dad is from Goshen, Indiana. So in the mid 90s/early 90s my dad— or like early 90s my dad was in Haiti on a mission's trip and my mom's family was hosting him. And they like hit it off and then he like left because he had to come back to the US. And then he went back to Haiti again for another mission's trip, and I don't know he started dating my mom and then they got married. And so my parents moved to central Illinois where my grandparents were living, in a small town called Tuscola which has about 800-ish people, I don't know it's like an hour north-ish of Peoria. So after while my parents were kind of like, "*Well, we're kind of done with this area. . .*" and so my parents were like, "*Let's go be missionaries in Haiti.*" And so (I don't know this was like around 2014) so it was me and my two brothers and my parents moved to Haiti for about six months in 2014. And then we moved back to the United States and we were like, "*Well where do we end up?*" And my dad's like, "*I used to live in Evanston for like five years.*" when he was like 3 to 8 he lived in Evanston, so my parents were like, "*Let's move to Evanston.*" So here I am.

I would say my experiences at Evanston Township High School were mostly positive. I don't know. . . I guess I met a lot of great, great people across all lines: faculty. . . staff. . . students, that have really helped me grow and mature and kinda create the person I am today. I've had a lot of teachers that really kind of pushed me and my boundaries to kind of force me to like look at new things. Like my first semester here I had art first period with Mr. Simos, and I didn't really like art that much but Mr. Simos pushed me, and I kind of grew a little bit. And like taking ceramics with Ms. Seibold second semester— I honestly really didn't know what to expect from ceramics, I was like, "*Oh we're making pottery. . . I don't know about this.*" But by the end of the semester I definitely enjoyed doing it and Ms. Seibold remembers this, but like I used to come in, in the mornings, like every morning before school I would come in at like eight and do the extra half-hour and I was like way ahead at one point. And I think that there was like a solid week where I was so far ahead that there was nothing for me to do. So I did "Free Clay Day" for a week straight, and I'd load the kiln a lot. So there's a lot of that.

I came in sophomore year and it was like an adjustment that was hard for like a week– so when I lived in Haiti, I went to a missionary school which was like 200 kids for K through 12, and the building was laid out very differently. It was a very open campus so you went from like building to building, almost like a college campus layout in the sense that you were outdoors a lot like you didn't just stay in the high school like a typical US high school, you were moving from building to building. So it's a lot different than here. So adjusting to that threw me off for a little bit, also the building being ginormous! So I was like, "*Uhh where do I go?*" and so there was all that.

Towards the beginning of this year, a safety officer stopped me as I was trying to leave for service and he was like, *"Where is your ID?"*. Everybody else had said to safety officers that were in Senior Studies, and that they're going right over there to meet with their teacher. And he stopped me and he was like, *"Well I need some ID."* and then when other kids in class walked by, being a white kid and he just let them through and it took me to the point of pointing him out– pointing out his racial profiling of me, essentially that's what it is. It was also just surprising that I was racially profiled by a minority. But that was a more negative experience here.

There's some other experiences I have this year, from Senior Studies. It was another service time, we were leaving for service first semester, I was— the car that we were all. . . the car that my service group was taking to District 65 was in the front and so we were walking from the back to the front and it was me and three other people, and two of them were white females and one of them was a Latina female. And so we're walking through the halls and they're like, *"Oh we're in Senior Studies."* And so we're walking and they're just like letting them through and the safety officer stopped me and forced me to take a tardy slip even though I was leaving the building. And so I started complaining and I was like, *"I mean I'm leaving the building, I'm leaving with them, you can clearly see all of us together, can I just go?"* And luckily one of the other safety officers took the tardy away for me because he knew what was up, but it was really annoying that the safety officer was heckling me.

In my time here I guess I've learned. . . just be yourself and work hard, respect others and your high school and going here you will generally have no problems. I'm not going to say you're not gonna have any problems, because you just will. But if you come in with the right attitude, and you work hard and you don't try to be someone you're not, your high school career will be generally a good experience.

As a whole, you see this in the microcosm of ETHS, but as a whole— well Evanston and ETHS are both very diverse in a sense, but you don't— you don't really see people intermingle a lot, outside of the races very often, like you do see it to a certain extent but really mostly it's the white people go with the white people, the black people go to black people the Latinx people with Latinx people, the Middle Eastern stay together. . . the eastern Asian/Pacific islanders. . . they just all kind of stick together. And Evanston kind of groups them– I don't know how intentional it is anymore, obviously at one point it was intentional (I don't know however many years ago) but even though we may not really be trying to do that, like you definitely can see it if you walk in the cafeteria you don't see tables with six different races sitting together, generally. So I'd just like seeing a growth in that, make people of different backgrounds, across all scales: religion, race, sexuality, gender, whatever, kind of intermingling more. That's probably the biggest thing I want Evanston to do.

So my project is, I make a weekly podcast on ETHS on sports called "Wildkit Weekly" where I present scores from the previous week, I interview athletes and coaches on their perspective sports, and sort of just talk with them about topics that sort of relate to their sports. Like concussions and women's soccer or something like that. Just to see their take on it and kind of talk with about their sports, really. My first one who was with Nojel Eastern and Leighah Wool, the one that's coming up this week, I interviewed Elena Hart for soccer, I interviewed Alyssa for bowling. . .

Tim Brewer

My father was born in Allentown, Pennsylvania. And my mom was born in Delavan, Wisconsin and they ended up here because my dad ended up going to Kellogg Business School, so they moved here while he went there. I think they liked— they kind of realized that it was an up-and-coming suburb just cause it's right next to Chicago. When they moved here there was like no restaurants or bars. Then by the time that they-like when my brother was born they saw like restaurants and stuff popping up and they saw that it was kind of becoming a good suburb. And it had like good schools so I guess that they just like stayed.

Yeah, I liked high school, *laughs* it was fun. Freshman year was different because it was like a big change from middle school. I like the opportunities here I like how you can just do so many different things. Like you can do whatever you want, there's a club for it and like everything. I do a lot of things outside of school from sports to like cooking and stuff, hanging out with my friends. . . I don't know, there's just things for everybody. It's not even just stuff that I do, it's just like that everyone is involved, like everyone kinda found their own niche in high school, especially by senior year.

I went to Washington, I liked Washington a lot, it was fun. I was in the TWI program, loved it, it's the greatest thing I've ever done, like that's the greatest program. So it's like I grew up thinking that all of my classes for the rest of my life we're going to be half Latino. Like all of my friends were Latino and spoke Spanish and stuff and like I was always at Mexican barbecues and stuff, oh my god it was so fun. But then I got to middle school and it was like really different— it was just weird transitioning from the TWI program and being like *"Oh this is what it's actually like."* because I don't know it seemed to separate. Because when you were in elementary school you didn't know but when everyone got to middle school people unknowingly separated into— I don't want to say all the white kids hung out to-gether but they kind of did.

It's depressing to go outside of Evanston when you see how nor-mal close minded people are, whereas Evanston seems to be very liberal. I've traveled outside enough to realize that the rest of the world is not like that. I just think it's interesting that we're kind of sheltered from the close mindedness of the rest of the world. Be-ing surrounded by so many people and not even like— like I think the TWI program was a good example, like how I had no idea that anything was different— like Evanston is kind of a bubble where you don't run into any close minded people to change the way you think about things, like I thought that was normal. I like that, I don't know, you're just kinda more open minded growing up here.

I think everyone's worried about each other and not themselves, I think that that's a big thing, I think that people spend too much time (in Evanston I've noticed) stressing about other people. But they should just focus on themselves, not even in a mean way, I just think people should worry less about how other people live their own lives. So I think that everybody should just go about their business and enjoy themselves, and do whatever they like to do.

So for my project I making a cookbook, full of Cajun and Creole recipes, which is the style of food that I enjoy. There's a culture aspect and I'm trying to learn about the culture, and like the reason behind why they used specific ingredients, and like what cultures influenced those ingredients. Because like when the Spaniards colonized they brought this ingredient and like when the French colonized they brought this ingredient and it kinda formed a unique style of food. And that's kinda why I chose it, because it has its own culture, and it's the only place in the US with its own cuisine.

Catherine Cushing

My dad was born in Wildwood, which is like a small neighborhood in Chicago, this is actually my dad's shirt, my dad's softball shirt, the "Mealworms". And they'd meet— listen to how cute this is: his friend group was like called the "Mealworms", you know it's like the "FYG's", the "Flamingos". . . the "Mealworms", that kind of thing. And they like had a softball team and like did all this stuff together, and like a lot of them went to Loyola together and like a handful of them went to Notre Dame together, but not all of them. But still every. . . like 5 years they have a Mealworm reunion and they rent out, I dunno like a small lake house somewhere and just have a banger! And like they do it and it's like 30 guys, and now they're like 60 and they do it every year and it's so cute! So my dad— that's where he was born. And my mom was born in New Jersey, the Jersey Shore. . . and then my parents met at Loyola Law School, so in Chicago and then they ended up getting married and they wanted to stay around the area but didn't want to live in the city and they liked Evanston for all of the reasons we like to. . . whatever, you know. So they moved here.

So I was at Loyola— negative experience, in general. The year sucked. Loyola really didn't have any supports for me. I have a lot of issues, I need a lot of support and Loyola didn't do s*** for that. But coming to Evanston, when I was enrolling in the summer they set up this huge 504 meeting, there was a bunch of different people there, and yeah they just gave me a bunch of the accommodations I needed, and were super open to it. And every year we redo my 504 meeting just to kind of check in and now at this point there's probably seven or eight different adults of like different professions in the room but I get to run the meetings which has been really cool. Like if I'm assertive enough I just get to run through the checklist and be like "*I still need this accommodation because blah blah blah. . .*" and they trust me because when I don't need an accommodation I've spoken out about it. So that's been— that's worked out really well for me, I know it hasn't for everyone, I know people have had different experiences with it so I don't know what that necessarily pertains to but it's worked out really well for me so that's been something I've been really grateful for. Also, this is so generic, but I went to an all Catholic, predominantly white grade school K thru 8, and then Loyola. And coming here, there are a lot more discussions amongst the problems that exist here— there are positive discussions. So that was something that was new to me: being in a space where people are openly gay, openly trans, I just had never ever experienced that. So that was really a positive thing for me.

The first time I was ever in a predominantly black space was FAAM in 6th grade. And FAAM is Fellowship of African American Men, it's a basketball league that was started a long time ago to get the black men in the community doing something after school—

something positive. It's like a big community thing and its expanded, obviously, I'm not black or a man, but its expanded. It's a basketball league so they have a girls side and boys side, and I loved basketball and I started in 6th grade and I was like the only white person on my team, and it was just like so new to me. . . and I didn't have any like problem with it, it was just new to me. And at St. A's we had one black person in my class and like I knew him since I was little and like whatever— but this was the first time that I had been the only white person. I was in the minority and it was super interesting, and I was super uncomfortable with it, and I felt nothing to what black people feel when they're in all white situations, obviously. It was just really-really interesting to compare that, and then flip it and then add years and years of history and oppression on top of it. But I had a great time, a great experience. I made a lot of really really good friends who I'm still friends with now. So, I dunno that's kind of what I think of a lot when I think of the Evanston community, I just think back to like FAAM and that was such a positive part of the community, for me and for everyone in it. And historically— its really cool! The founders speak at the FAAM banquet every year and they're really cool. So that's one thing I like to think about— that's a positive experience in the community.

Also— I remember after the death of Dajae Coleman, the way that the community came together. . . it shouldn't have to take that for the community to come together, but, that's something that's always stuck with me.

I think that just because we have a diverse community numbers-wise we like hold ourselves on a pedestal above other communities. When in reality there's so much more work and conversations to be done here, and I think we think because on the outside it looks diverse and liberal that we are exempt from all these preconceived. . . like inborn racism and all this stuff (I'm talking about the white community right now). And I think that there are big problems at New Trier and I think in some aspects we are ahead of New Trier, at the same time there are places where we are at ground zero just as much. Looking at the white community, I think we tokenize the diversity that we have here and I think we tokenize friends we have that are people of color. And not on purpose obviously, but kind of use that to be like *"Oh. . . I'm woke."* I think "woke"— that's it: that's my biggest problem with Evanston. It's like a woke-off. First of all that word is just like— "woke". .? Like what do you mean, "woke"? Like that should just be being a human being. But I think it's become white people competing to see who can look the most socially aware, when in reality that's work we should be doing within ourselves before we put ourselves out there and act like we know what we're talking about! Yeah. . . I think I want the word "woke" to be erased from our vocabulary.

I'm gonna take away a lot from being in Evanston, but I think one thing I'm going to take away from is that. . . I feel like— so I have a lot of mental health disabilities. I suffer from depression. . . bipolar. . . whatever ADHD, anxiety, PTSD all that s***. And I feel like for a while I not knowingly used that as a way to feel like I a was super oppressed, marginalized person and in some respects, I mean like yeah mental health is super stigmatized and like yes sexual assault— I am a victim of sexual assault, and that is a problem a lot of women and people face. And like I'm gonna hold that close to my heart, like that's something that will always be a part of me, like there's work to be done there. But as a white woman I feel like I've realized that I'm not as oppressed as I like to think that I am. . . and I'm not as like, held back in the community as I like to think that I am, that's just me being lazy. I dunno and wanting to use hardships in my life as something that like, *"Oh that's why I'm doing bad in school."* or *"That's why I feel uncomfortable in this situation."* When in reality, yeah those are hard things that happened but compared to people of color and people of different identities, who've faced the same things as me. . . I dunno I guess I'm taking away I need to get the f*** off my high horse and like I dunno. . . I'm privileged as s***, that's what it is. I'm privileged as s*** and having bad things happen doesn't take away from my inborn privilege

So for my project I'm focusing on how trauma and oppression in inner city neighborhoods, especially in Chicago, affects the crime rates and violence, and I'm focusing that especially on juveniles. So kind of looking at the cycle of violence and the role that trauma plays in that cycle, and then I'm looking at how our criminal justice system and our juvenile justice system addresses the crime rather than the trauma, that I believed caused the crimes. And then I'm looking at ways in which the community— like what my outlook on community responsibility is (to provide services and resources and educate themselves about trauma rather than just using corrections as a form of punishment) and that kind of thing. So I'm interviewing a bunch of different people from different. . . kind of, sides of this, of the juvenile justice system. So I've interviewed a juvenile prosecutor, so someone who sends juveniles to prison for a living, which was. . . interesting. I interviewed some public defenders.

I interviewed Rick Hutt, who was the defense attorney in the Eric Morse case, he was the lawyer for Tykes and Jesse, who were the defendants, which was really interesting! And now he's the head of the public defender's office. I interviewed Judge Sheehan she's a judge in the juvenile court but also, more importantly, we interviewed about— she's creating a restorative justice court that focuses solely on taking crimes that would normally go to court and instead figuring out ways, through like peace circles and like community gatherings, to like, they call it "repairing the harms" without any type of record. Yeah, it's really cool and it looks like it's gonna get off the ground pretty soon. So that was a super interesting interview.

I interviewed a social worker at the Moran Center, some lawyers at the Moran Center. This man, he goes by "Fenom", he's a spoken word poet and a rapper and he works at Family Focus, and I interviewed him. He does a lot for restorative justice in the community, and anti-violence. So, yeah, I've just been talking to a lot of different people. And then I'm— so I've recorded all those interviews, and when I'm listening through them I pull out quotes that I think are specific— like very powerful or show a very specific point of view, on one side or another side of the issue. And I'm going to compile them and play them for different focus groups of people so like children (we haven't really figured it out yet) but like some kids, some adult and we want to do different socioeconomic classes, different races. . . and then each person is going to have a different piece of white paper and they are going to draw or write down what the different quotes made them feel, and then I'm going to compile them all into some type of collage. So, that's super all over the place, but that's basically what I'm working on right now.

Lauren Davis

Ok, so, my father was born here, in Evanston. And my mother was born in a place called Middletown, New York and she moved here when she was 25 I believe, to be with my dad. My dad's mom is from a place called Evansville, Indiana which is kind of south of here but it's like, Mason-Dixon line border so they considered themselves Southern. My dad's father is from here, so— I don't know the lineage after that but I know I'm at least 2nd generation Evanston.

My freshman year was hard because, the transition from 8th grade to high school was really difficult for me and my grandfather also passed away the winter of my freshman year so there was just a lot of changes with my family and stuff, that was making it hard for me to really focus on school. But even looking back. . . freshman year was like, nothing *laughs* but it felt so hard at the time. But, I think freshman year was like, a good year. . . socially. I liked the people I was hanging out with and I was having fun. We're not friends now but I don't regret any of the things that we did together and we still had fun while we were friends. Sophomore year was the same thing. Junior year was really hard because I had a lot of mental health stuff going on and I was taking the AP English and History block— a f***ing disaster. And I was pressuring myself to keep my grades up for college applications and stuff. But, I don't know, I think I've had really mixed experiences here. I've had some really shitty days and some really good ones. But I definitely think this is one of the best places to experience high school, because we have so much that other people don't get to experience until they're like in college or grown and we have all these resources and all these different kinds of people that are here, available to us.

I did go to a District 65 school. I went to— I actually went to preschool in CPS and then I came here. I don't remember much, I just remember my preschool classroom being really crowded. There was a lot of kids. But my kindergarten class was actually— there were like, two separate classes but we shared this big classroom. So it was kind of the same. . . but it felt different because I went from being with mostly kids of color to mostly white kids and Asian kids. Cause I went to Walker, that's like in Skokie so. . . yeah. But from what I can remember it was a good experience education wise, because I was kind of able to find the things that I liked to learn and the things I wanted to like, focus on. Because middle school education is so generic like you don't learn anything unless you really want to learn specific things. So that taught me like, "*Maybe you can Google the answer as to like why they left this certain thing out of textbooks.*" or whatever. Which was cool. Middle school sucked, socially. I went to Chute. I would never go back there even if you paid me a million dollars. That was mostly because— I just didn't like it because middle schoolers are so gross. Everybody is so clique-y and mean and bullies and stuff. Yeah, so it was, ah it was awful. You could not pay me to be thirteen again. But, I think I did better here than I would somewhere else.

And then, Evanston-wise, like because of my grandparents and my dad— they had a family business for a really long time, that was a transportation company, so they had like the big charter busses and like the town cars and driving people to the airport and so everybody kind of knew them and knew who I was (and also because of my church too). So it's always felt really homey, not only because I'm from here but like everyone I know is here and we all know each other. So I had a really big community experience in Evanston and I don't know if everyone has that, but mine has definitely been like, I know my neighbors and like. . . yeah.

I mean, I think there's prejudice everywhere. I mean, like even in District 65 schools; my teachers expecting me to not do as well in my classes. . . or like, remember when we had to like— you would leave your reading class or whatever and you had to sit and read a page while they timed you or something? And they would be like, *"Oh my gosh, you're so articulate, you read so well!"* I'd be like. . . *"Yeah. . ?* I was always really good at reading, like I guess I read fast or whatever but they were just like, *"You're so...articulate, you read so well!"* and I'd be like, *"I'm not illiterate like I don't know what you were expecting but thanks."*

There's been definitely more prejudice in the summers because you could go wherever and I would go the Y a lot with my siblings or my friends and we would go to the lake and stuff, and just kind of watching as I got older, noticing how older white women would be cautious as I was walking across the street with my brother and my dad. Or like, being followed in the store. Like I was followed in Urban Outfitters one time when I was like 13 with my group of friends. There's like, one time my brother (he's older than me so he's already graduated) and I was like a sophomore I think, and he came to see Ms. Joyce and I had gym at the same time— but I didn't know he was here. And I was walking towards the west wing gym doors and he like ran up from behind me and jumped on my back so I was like *jokingly*, *"What the f***?"* and we just started fighting in the middle of the hallway and this woman runs out of her classroom—

this white woman, like out of nowhere and she's like, *"SIR, GET OFF HER, GET OFF HER, I'LL CALL SAFETY! blah blah blah. . ."* making a whole scene but like, everyone around us like— it's clear that we're just playing like we're laughing while we're hitting each other like nobody is in danger or anything. And like, the way that she just I don't know, assumed that I was in danger because this big black man is with me. Just, I don't know, it was just really weird. But like, little stuff like that has happened all the time. But nothing that's ever made me want to like, leave.

I think I always been very aware that I was black and that there are certain ways that people will look at me because of that. But I didn't really start paying attention until I was about 14 or 15. . . Like not Trayvon Martin but I think Mike Brown was the one right after that, like the one that blew up and um, I was just like, all of the sudden really aware of like the people around me and the way they thought and the way that they spoke to each other. Like I would always hear my dad talking about how like there's two different Evanston's, but I didn't really understand and then I started experiencing meeting people in high school like, they were white and they would be totally cool. And then my dad always asks like *"Who's their parents?"* and then he would be like *"Oh. . ."* like he knew something that I didn't know. And so like just growing up to find out like, my science teacher in middle school. . . worked on the Trump campaign just like stuff like that. Just stuff like that that you don't notice— you don't care when your little. Like nobody's worried if you're a Republican or Democrat or whatever. But now that this is real stuff that affects me and I'm conscience about, you just start to notice all the weird things from the people that you didn't pay attention to before.

I think living here's made me check my privilege a lot. . . because Evanston is really like this super suburb on one hand, like once you pass Isabella and you get to the other side of Evanston and you go by the lake and stuff, it's like, just any other white suburb: picket fence, big houses, 2 kids and whatever. There's also the side of Evanston that's Section 8 housing, and like, everyone is not. . . I've been fortunate enough to have both of my parents in my life, up until now both of my parents have had stable jobs and stuff and so like

I've never really had to worry about any of these things until like I've been making friends with people who like, can't just call their dad to pick them up because they feel like it. Or can't just drop $20 for all their friends to eat at McDonalds or whatever. And also because my mom's family— she's biracial, so. . . my first cousins on my mom's side are all white because all of her siblings married a white spouse and had white kids and they live in like rural places so when I go up there it's like. . . I know that I am black. No matter where I go I am still black. And then there's times when like, my dad's family, my cousins from the city or whatever come up and they're like "*Oh Lauren, driving around in her own car blah blah blah.*" Like I'm so privileged that there's shit that like, I don't even think about like, I don't know, it's almost like I'm split in half but, that's just the way that I grew up.

I think definitely just learning how to take everything with a grain of salt. Because there's so many different kinds of people here that you get to learn something from someone. And there's so many different cultures that you get to authentically experience. But there's also a lot of different sides to every story and I think just knowing that just because like, someone is like me, like they might look like me or whatever doesn't mean that we have the same experience.

I wish that people took the time to kind of have— not necessarily the Evanston unit we had in Senior Studies but kind of just had more of a general knowledge of like, why Evanston is the way it is, like especially with all of the redlining and stuff that has happened. . . And you have a white women trying to run of 5th Ward Alderman, like *"What are you doing you don't know what's best for the 5th ward!"* I dunno I just feel like there's so many people who live in East Evanston or North Evanston who like— they don't have any reason come over here. So like, they don't really know anything other than what they hear and what they assume. And then there's people here who are like *"Nah, f*** white people, like they never do anything for me, they're all bad."* And that's not the case either. So I just wish they would take the time to learn each other's sides.

I also think that there's— remember that article we read on the guy who said *"There's just enough crime to keep things entertaining."* It's the people like that— it's the white people like that: who can live close to the lake where they have their own stretch of private beach but like will also be like "*Oh yeah this guy just got shot in my neighborhood the other day!*" or whatever. But they like, I don't know, it's built so that we don't' have to know anything about the other side. But like, it's weird, not to. Because then you don't get to experience the whole Evanston. It's supposed to be, like, you're supposed to have a little black kid who has 5 other siblings and a single mom that lives all in a one-bedroom apartment. You're supposed to have that kid be friends with the kid whose dad is like the president of Northwestern, it's supposed to be like that, and it's not.

So my project— I'm doing a shadow of my pastor and I'm exploring what it's like to be a young woman in Christian ministry which is like really heavily male dominated. And that kind of turning into me exploring rape culture on the church and "Womenism" which is kind of black-feminism but also tied in with religion.

Annie Doyle

I think it be easier to go parent by parent: so my dad was born in Washington DC and he moved around a lot when he was a kid and then he went to college in DC and then he went to grad school, where he met my mom and that was at University of Missouri. And my mom was born in Evanston actually, but then she moved to Des Moines, Iowa and she was like five and went to school there. . . high school there, and then she met my dad, and then they got married three years after college. And then they moved to Chicago and lived there for about like five years before they started having kids and they wanted to move to Evanston for like I guess the schools, and the houses were cheaper than the apartments in Chicago. . .

I mean back then they were. . . probably not as much anymore *laughs* but yeah.

I think I really liked high school because middle school (towards the end) my friends— we like dissipated, we all like went in different directions and then we were like able to find new places within what we wanted to do. And it's also interesting, senior year you find yourself going back to those friends that you kind of dissipated from freshman year and then you kinda come back together. So that was cool! And I know that this is kind of like the cliché that people say about the high school but like there is so much that you can do, like there's a lot of different clubs or whatever. I really found a home in the newspaper. I think it's really like, a fun thing to stay connected to what's happening in our school and not only write about it but like show— portray it to the student body at large, and I found a really great home in that. One of my favorite stories was on the new disciplinary policies in the school. It's like the model of "restorative justice", instead of like immediately going to suspension or expulsion. They kind of work with like an advisory team or something, and it like helps the student come up with a plan in order to reverse their behavior, or reverse the problem they're having. And it employs the Peer Jury a lot more. Which I think is really helpful because it helps students come together and solve problems as like a team. And that something I think a lot of students don't think about, like the majority of students who aren't getting in trouble a lot don't think about the way discipline works here and they don't think about the way it can be changed and made better for every student. I think it's so easy to think about the restorative justice thing on a national scale like in the prison system, which is obviously happening, but like you could also do it in small scales like in your community.

I think I've always had like a lot of different communities I've been a part of, which is nice. I was really lucky to always have like a summer camp or whatever, and that always made it feel like there was a community outside of school which was nice. And I always liked elementary school, I thought it was fun because I think my teachers were really happy about what they were doing. I went to

Dewey and I think that that school is really good as the teachers seemed really knowledgeable about what they were teaching and I can reflect on that now having learned about teaching more and like having learned what makes a good teacher, I can see how I was really lucky to of gone to such a good school.

I think TWI and Gen-Ed was separated for some reason. I don't know why because like we were all the same age and in the same grade and it's just weird that like some of them– I think like for example: Tessa Otting and like Ruth Osterreicher, they were in my grade and went to Dewey, but I didn't really know them until six grade. And I think that's so strange, and there's other people like Chyna Wright, like she was in TWI and I didn't know her until like middle school started. We went to the same school for like six years, and it's just strange and I don't know why that is that they're just not like part of the regular school for some reason.

I feel like a lot of the prejudice in Evanston is kind of like micro stuff and it's easy to just like shake off. I think one of the biggest things that I've noticed is like the different police interactions, like a lot of people of color— like I've seen the video on the dash cam. And I feel like before, it was really easy being in this community that's kind of seemingly utopic, to think that like police brutality is just something that happens in like southern states or like other parts of the country but like the racial problems that are happening all across the country are happening here too. It's not like we're unique because we live in a state that goes mostly blue with like elections and stuff. We have like the same systemic problems with like police abuse and all that stuff. And that was definitely an eye-opening thing because it's easy to just like look at those videos and think of it as just a hashtag but it happens in your own community.

I think I definitely have an Evanston identity, I think we definitely have this sense of. . . I don't know if superiority is the right word, but like over other suburbs. We're like *"Oh we're not like those weird people from Wilmette. . . we're Evanston."* Whatever that means. And I feel like no matter how far (this might sound really-really corny) but I feel like no matter how far people move away or even if they stay here, you'll always like feel connected to those people. . . for some reason? I think that the weird kind of perception that this town has and also like the reality of it makes you like super knowledge-able about it and feel more close to it.

I think I would like to see more acknowledgement of the fact that we mirror the rest of the country pretty much. Like we may have– like in terms of political problems, and terms of racial problems, in terms of like all that stuff. . . Evanston may be better from a marketing standpoint point, like we "look" better. Like we at least don't out-wardly say these things. But like I want there to be more acknowl-edgement that these problems exist in our town, and these prob-lems need to be acknowledged in our town and dealt with. Not just say "*We're better than a town in Alabama*". . . Like we obviously are *laughs* but we may not be. Like our history has the same lineages those towns do and just because we've evolved in this like liberal way, we haven't really made change for the people who need it.

I wanted to focus on environmental education because I think like the only way stuff about climate change is going to change is if we like educate the younger generation about it and if they feel motivated to change it they're going to hopefully do it. So I'm writ-ing a children's book about oceanic environmental problems, about like how when— it not only hurts the planet but it like hurts com-munities when the planet is under attack or whatever from pollution, overfishing and like the polar ice caps melting. It not only affects the chemistry of the planet but it also really hurts people's lives. I think they know about it and that climate change is real, they just don't know how to fight in their own way.

Nick Erhart

Evanston Township High School itself— I have really enjoyed. I feel like when I hear about what's going on at other high schools I'm always like, so surprised because that's like definitely not what ETHS is like! But. . . yeah, I really like it. It's really different here because of the variety of choices and types of people we have here. People talk about how it's a bubble, but I kinda like that bubble because the outside world is scary. And while there's issues here it's still better than other places.

Like I said before I feel like Evanston is really different from other communities, even compared to the communities along the North Shore. I think we're very open and accepting compared to many places, and so different from so many places we are relatively close to, like the northern suburbs. I definitely wouldn't want to live anywhere else— like whenever I visit another place I get depressed because. . . I like *really* wouldn't want to live there. But yeah I like Evanston, it's a town with city vibes and people who aren't a******s. It has shaped me into a better person just because of the people who I've been able to be surrounded by. And I feel like as I've grown up— and gotten older and older, I have become a much more accepting person, just because I've grown up here.

So, I am making a documentary on the Refugee Crisis. And I'm interviewing people who have been involved and am using that information to make a film. The documentary will consist of my own work. . . and the documentary isn't mainly about the people who I interview, but their interviews have added to my project to provide context. It's basically a documentary that I'm trying to make look professional with the time that I have. It's going to be on how the Refugee Crisis affects various people. . . and how it affects people in places like Evanston, and also my own commentary on it. The footage is of a variety of protests, like I got footage of a protest at Northwestern. . . protests at O'Hare, the final family to enter Chicago before the executive order was passed. . . footage of museums, I also have footage from online which consists of footage of refugees original homes, and holding places. . . eye opening footage that a lot of people haven't seen yet.

Hazel Filmore-Brady

My dad was born and raised here, so that's probably why I'm back here! My mom grew up in Buffalo Grove, Illinois and then they both lived in Chicago. I actually lived in like Lincoln Square until I was like 9, before I ended up moving here. I have a lot of family here, all of my dad's brothers live here with their kids, and my grandma did. . . and so I think that was the draw to living in Evanston. And I think it was also the school system, and the high school.

Alright, this will sound cliché but Evanston's greatest asset is definitely the diversity. And I think I really value that a lot and tried to take advantage of that, in my high school career. So I've been a part of— this is kind of funny, this is what I wrote about for my college essay, but the cross country team and the track team have been like huge communities for me in high school. And what's interesting is that the cross country team is like entirely white and the track team is almost all African Americans. So that's been really interesting and just like such a big part of high school has been those two communities and really seeing the contrast between them. They could not have been more different— also every school in Chicago, everyone who runs cross country runs track, like it's like a thing. And at Evanston there are like 100 girls on cross country and like three of us run track. . . and it's definitely because of cultural differences. And if you look at every sport, like they all have their demographics. I think being a part of those communities led me to recognize what Evanston's bigger weaknesses is, which is that we're diverse but so segregated, so that would be like the negative side of my high school experience here. I think you see— you walk into a classroom and you all look like each other, like myself included I'm being a total hypocrite here— sit with people who look like them and act like them. I feel like I'm gonna look back and see so many missed opportunities. And in Senior Studies you really reflect on that, and like think *"Oh my god I could have taken advantage of this diversity so much more than I actually did."*

I think that interacting with difference is just the most— I think just like the idea that people change people and the relationships you build and like interacting with different people is like the most important thing in life. Period. It's just like talking and having dialogue with other people, and building relationships with interesting— and I'm not just talking about diverse like race, like I went to a 3,500 kid high school, and I'm so grateful for that because it led me to talk to so many different kinds of people.

I love the focus of your project because I'm talking about how diverse we are and how we're like *"Oh we're so consciously and activist-y!"* but it's like so— not even a little bit and it's very fake— a lot of it. So I think acknowledging that and bringing forth the history— I love that, that's awesome. And making Evanston more authentic and less in denial of its issues so that people can actually address those issues, like segregation issues. I think there's a large, elite, white class within Evanston that's just not acknowledging any of what's going on.

So for my project I am getting involved in the immigration movement. So I am looking at what ETHS specifically— ETHS community, including: teachers, students, administration. . . can do to be more supportive of undocumented students. So I've been interning in Pilsen, the Resurrection Project, which is a really neat organization which works— well they do a lot of stuff! But their immigration department works on educating people about— undocumented people about what their rights are and help them apply for citizenship and DACA and stuff like that. My focus has become kind of— I kind of like what you said earlier "*I was doing this research which made me so angry and I just wanted to like have everybody know.*" like that's exactly how I feel— like so much outrage. So I did like a survey of like teachers and students like "*Can undocumented students go to college?*" and like "*Can they apply for financial aid?*" you know— DACA, stuff like that. I was shocked at how little— I kind of expected students not to know a lot but like teachers don't know anything, and that was frustrating for me. And so I think what I'm going to try and do is a presentation to teachers specifically, but also students just kind of raising awareness about this issue. I think people don't know how difficult it is to be undocumented and there are so many struggles that come along with that and college is just one piece of that.

We have the DREAMERS club at ETHS and they're awesome and I only just found out about them this year and— which I just feel terrible about. And I've been getting more involved with that. You just come in— I think there's a different focus depending on what immediate goals there are, there's a lot of fundraising so they'll be like "*Hang out and go pick out t-shirt designs!*" It's very chill. . . it's very— I think, largely about creating a supportive environment.

Like right now Trump might be abolishing DACA which is like. . . the scariest thing ever. Assuming that you know what it is (you would be surprised like 80% of people in my survey did not even— like hadn't even heard of it which was kind of scary) but it's like what allows undocumented people to attend school. Right now Evanston is a sanctuary city, which means. . . I'm not totally sure, but basically the city will not be disclosing the status of its people, it will be protecting against ICE raids which are legit scary things that happen. And like our school is a sanctuary school now which means that if like (what's scary is that this is an actually very real threat) it's like if immigration authorities or ICE were to come like knocking on our door, our school is a safe space so it can't turn over a student, they will be safe within our school. Actually I don't know a lot about what it means to be a sanctuary city, in all honesty and like what that entails. And I think to be honest it can't do a lot. . . which is sad.

Hugo Flores

My parents were born in Mexico and they decided to come here because family happened to live here and it was part of us like. . . finding a better life.

Coming to ETHS, I was really afraid, just going through a lot of different experiences. Just like, it shook me. But like as you become part of the community, even if you don't want to, it just kind of happens. You start to see that people appreciate you, and you appreciate others, and it's just like, it's so nice. . . sometimes you feel like you're alone in such a big place, you've never, like as a teen, you've never been in like, such a big place. And you just like see a lot of different faces, who you won't ever like, say *"Hi."* to. . . and others who you're just going to have stuck in your head the whole time when you leave high school.

So I joined District 65 when I came here in second grade, I went to Washington. And it was really hard getting used to the whole, "Welcome to America" situation, and I have a hard time trying to find who I belonged with. So I stayed with people who looked like me and acted like me— well I stayed with the Latinx kids, I felt comfortable with them. . . and I was just trying to get used to the language and the culture. I was in the TWI program— it really did help me to speak English, by the age of fifth grade I was able to have fully functioning English conversations. And it was a lot easier to understand what was going on around me. But it was through a lot of help and a lot of teachers who are able to help me get where I am.

But Nichols was another mess, because I got into a depression because I didn't appreciate who I was. It was a period of time. . . like, my parents separated and nothing really was going well. I didn't like myself, I hated who I was, I hated who I pretended to be. I almost— I tried to go and— I physically harmed myself. And that led to a lot of pain. What it comes down to, what I got out of Nichols is that you got to keep moving forward. Because even though life hits you a lot, with road blocks and with scary thoughts, you can get through. It's also something that I was able to finalize and learn here at ETHS, which is you have to speak about your experience, so that others who are going through the same thing aren't afraid. So that they don't feel like they're alone and so they don't feel like they're the only one going through the same thing that you went through. High school was just such a mess, from losing countless, countless family members to seeing how the world is around me, but you meet great people here. They're hidden between the crowd but, but once you get to meet them you're amazed at what they have done, and it sadly happened in the last year of my high school experience, where I met so many amazing people. People who are just finding themselves and their identity to people that already have a goal in life are going to push for it. And it's just really amazing to finally get to meet people like these.

I've seen people in Evanston have racial encounters a lot. I remember after the Black Lives Matter protest that happened in Evanston last summer, me and some people went to get food and as we sat down, we enjoyed ourselves and we enjoyed our company. It was clear that we just came from the protest, we had the Black Lives Matter gear, we were dressed alike, so it was clear, and this man came up to us and asked, "*Why does it matter? Why do black lives matter suddenly?*" I felt really conflicted because this man just came up and said that the experiences that happened is invalid. And it's just like when you look at the TV and you see the news, you see the horrible atrocities that were happening.

I feel like the only change that I would like to see in Evanston— it's like everyone says that we appreciate diversity and we will push for equality yet we see the housing, and we see our segregation. You go to South Evanston and you see a lot of lower income families living there, and you go up north or towards the Lakeside and you see mansions, beautiful, beautiful houses. And you see all the social and economic imbalances that exist here. The school requires reduced lunch, and many students come from families which of been broken from like shootings, no would like to talk about that side of Evanston. The side that still has homeless people downtown, and still gets called the most liberal cities in the US. It's kind of scary. Because Evanston is a big liberal bubble, and we promote change all around, but we still haven't changed ourselves, that's the big scary thing here.

So my project is talking about the education system of Illinois. I'll be comparing two schools, one in a higher income area and one in a lower income area of Illinois. And showing how taxes and all of this influences a lot of what resources students get and in general talking about how some teachers don't push students toward success in the same way that they push other students to success. And connecting that will be— so something happened in the middle of my project, I was really hoping to get this 45-minute presentation going, talking about this because I'm very passionate about education. But I have some circumstances that don't allow me to be a teacher, so I really can't finish the first part of my project. So I decided to talk about the

"American Dream" because that something that I've been told that I had to push for. And I've been told to go for the American Dream because, because that's the only way that it will make the sacrifice worth it. But my American Dream is not gonna happen. And that's the experience for a lot of people like me. But if I can just get that idea out there, that the American Dream isn't for everyone, and that there's a lot of different American Dreams, not just the one that is pushed by the media, I'll be happy with that and that's what I'm pushing for my Senior Studies project.

Sam Garry

I live with my mom, but my mom was born in Houston, Texas and we moved here because she was studying shiatsu at this place and there's a shiatsu clinic in Evanston, and she wanted to study there. And we liked Chicago and stuff so, we liked the lake, you know…

Well I moved here freshman year, and in terms of my experience in high school: it was really welcoming, like everyone was really nice. I've never experienced— I've never seen bullying or any of that type of stuff, like outright bullying. Everyone seems pretty welcoming and accepting of other people. That's what I experienced when I came here, and that's what I've experienced ever since.

I came from Colorado, which is like— in terms of race and

stuff. . . only white people, and like Latino people. It wasn't like cul-ture shock it was just a different group of people. Like there are a lot more Black people and Asian people here, so in terms of race there's that. . . but. . . it's a lot different from Colorado. Like in Colo-rado, where I came from, I came from Boulder which is just like a lot of really rich— I guess they're rich here too, but a lot of really rich, like white people that are really obsessed with like exercising and like yoga. There are a lot of like trust fund hippies like going to yoga. . . running in spandex. . . there are a lot of like biker people in Boulder. And then here it's a lot more city like, there's a lot more diversity— like there's a lot of people of different backgrounds and such. I think it's because we're so close to Chicago, so there's a lot of cultures from there, which I think is cool.

I know like, people will have prejudice when they're like cracking jokes or things, and I don't think they mean to be like, having preju-dice but like people make stereotypical jokes about other races or other genders. I haven't experienced any out-right prejudice in per-son, where people are being just outright a**hole.

I definitely want to see less segregation for the neighborhoods. I think that's one of the main issues in Evanston cause— yeah, people always talk about how diverse we are, but really. . . are we really that diverse? Because we're all living in separate areas and such. Also, I don't like that the beaches aren't free. . . I think they could improve the busses *laughs* I don't drive so I rely on busses a lot, like lots of times I like, get out of school early and I have no way to get home, I have no way to get anywhere from school, but like that makes sense because most people get out of school at one time.

For my project I'm just making music or I'm gonna make— I'm gonna interview people that are of all different ages and hopefully like— well different backgrounds. I'm gonna ask them about their lives and I'm gonna make an album where each song is like, a stage of life. And I'm gonna write the lyrics based on what people said in their interviews. I'll just ask questions like, "What is important to you?" and stuff, and a lot of teenagers would say that like school is important to them and like college. . . And then kids will say—

kids will just say like having fun. I'll ask them, *"What scares you?"*—the cool things is that like based on the ages there is usually like a theme, which is kind of the point I am trying to make. I was trying to show that like even though we're all so different we all still experience like, similar things and we all feel similar things. Like, when they were kids everyone was scared of the dark. . . and like everyone was really imaginative as kids or like would always play imagination games. . . like you probably did that and I know I did that. And like they were scared of monsters, ghosts and things. . . Then just like early adults have to face like, huge responsibilities, and like usually are struggling to like, make ends meet and such. So, those are some of the themes.

Gabby Gordon

My mom was actually born here, she lived in like Haiti for most of her childhood but she moved back here because her mom found a better job here. She like made more money than she did in Haiti and also her dad was here so. . . that's why she moved here. And then my dad was born here and chose to live here because his family lives here and he's close to his family.

ETHS is like I don't know. . . generally it's a high school, you know, and so like I had the regular high school experience: I had the ups and downs. Mostly I like everyone here, at ETHS. . . everyone's pretty cool, I haven't had any like bad experiences. I think everything's been normal here, I think senior year was kind of crappy just because of like the amount of work and stuff, but other than that everything's good. I think also senior year I started paying more attention to like who I'm around, like the different personalities and all that stuff. Generally, my experience here has been good.

For middle school I went to King Lab— I liked King lab, I liked how small it was. It was like a little community— a little family, there were little difficulties and separations within that. . . like the "Black Family" and all that stuff, like I don't know why that was a thing. I liked it though, everyone was pretty welcoming and nice and all that. . . I think in ETHS you're forced to be around each other more, but like District 65, depending on where you live it groups different people. . . different everything together. I don't know, that wasn't my experience cuz at King Lab I feel like it was pretty diverse and like everyone was pretty good with each other. But I see like how other schools in District 65 could be separated.

I think in the ETHS community a lot of kids can see it, that there's a little bit of a separation— I don't know a little bit— a lot a bit of separation! There's a lot of like exclusiveness among the grade, in like between different white people and black people— everybody. And just like getting together can be a problem, like parties and stuff, I don't know if I'm allowed to talk about that. . . But like at parties and stuff we'll go but then still like be separate and stuff at a party, and then there's like parties that a lot of groups of black people won't come to them because like they feel like they're— not like there was a specific chart of like who's invited, but like they assume already that they're not invited because of who's going. I also think there's a lot of cops pulling over kids cuz they "look suspicious" and all that stuff.

I think I'd like to see people be more involved in the community, and like being around each other. Instead of just saying that they want to be equal and around each other, but like actually having, I don't know, like more events in the community that we can all go to and stuff like that. . . community service. . . * laughs* but like yeah that type of stuff! But my project is "Humans of Evanston" And it's trying to get youth and the community more involved in giving back to the community. So I volunteered at different service sites and got to know a little bit about them, interviewed people, and posted stuff on social media where kids can see it and kind of got to know about the service sites around Evanston. And then I've also created surveys for kids to like fill out if they have done it or haven't done it, if they'd like to try it they can sign up. So I'll be like, next week, going to those sites and seeing how many of them show up and asking them if they would recommend a friend and do it again. . . that type of stuff. So just trying to advocate for youth and trying to get us to give back to the community, and us being together and doing stuff.

Sean Harris

My mom was born in New Jersey, and she moved to South Bend, because my grandpa got a job there, and then she lived there for a while and went to college at University of Chicago. And then from there moved to Evanston, actually after I was born, for like the better schools and stuff. And the same thing with my dad— well not the same thing with my dad, he was born in Hoffman Estates, and then moved to Park Ridge, went to Main South and then when I was born, moved to Evanston.

I mean, I really like ETHS, so far, it's a great group of people, everyone seems pretty accepting. I dunno I'm glad we have so many resources and opportunities, that the school provides. Yeah, I've never met someone at ETHS that's really not a fan of it— at least not anybody I know.

I dunno I've always liked Evanston, like as kid I've always liked to hang out at the parks, that's like the first thing that comes to mind, that was like one of my favorite things— like I would always go to Penny Park and like Mason Park and like play soccer and play on the wooden playground. So when they tore that down, I felt like part of me left when they tore Penny Park down. But I dunno, Evanston's a great place, the beaches are nice, I really haven't had a negative experience here, or something that would make me dislike it in anyway.

I guess living here has allowed me to be whoever I want to be. There's no like— well I guess there kinda is like a social norm you can fit into— like I just think of someone who's wearing like some Polo, some Vineyard Vines, riding around in their Jeep Wrangler with the top popped off in the summer or some s*** like. . . that, "*Going to a big sports school.*" But there's so many people who don't, so it makes it kinda— so you can just do whatever you want.

This is gonna sound kind of weird, but everything in Evanston— all these stores kind of close like really early, so if it's like past nine and you wanna get some food you really can't. So I guess I would rather have stores open later, like other than Andy's cuz like eating custard at 11 isn't a dinner. And you can't go to Burger King— I mean you *could* but it's not good food. So I guess that's one of the things that I would change, I dunno.

For my project I'm actually expanding on my business. . . called E-Town Pet Care, so I'm just trying to get a bunch— a lot more clients. And my goal is to raise $2,000 and then donate the money, because I can't keep any of the money, to the animal shelter.

Samantha Idler

My mom was born in the Philippines and her family moved to Berke-ley California when she was six months old, because her dad— they wanted a better life and her dad got a job with Pepsi and Budweiser in the states so. . . no, he got a job with Pepsi and he moved to Berkeley and then he got a job with Budweiser and they moved to Wisconsin. . . I don't know. And then my dad was born in Long Is-land. . . maybe. And they both went to University of Wisconsin and they both reconnected in Chicago. And I've moved seven times— I've only lived in Illinois and North Carolina but like it's always been different towns. So like I was born in Chicago and then I moved when I was six months old to like a place in North Carolina, and then

I moved to a different place in North Carolina and then I moved to Glen Ellyn which is like a western suburb. And then I move back to Chapel Hill and then I moved to Durham and then I moved here. Well I lived in the city for a short time but that doesn't really count. But I think we ended up in Evanston because they were choosing between Evanston and Wilmette and they just really didn't want to live in Wilmette. I think they like the community feel in Evanston a lot better.

So I moved here in eighth grade and I came from a school of 23 people, in North Carolina. So it was a really big transition even to Haven but then when I heard that ETHS just was like over 3000 kids, I was like really scared to come here and I was really scared that I was going to get lost. I think that overall my experience in Evanston has been really good. And I think that— I don't know I kinda attribute like a lot of the reason why ETHS just has benefited me a lot, to like the *Evanstonian*. I've been working with the paper since freshman year and I think that it's been like a good outlet to talk about the issues and talk about the problems and then also talk about realistic solutions and like, talk to administrators. I think that it's given me kind of a unique perspective. It's my first year writing opinion, and I was kind of scared to write opinion before, I kind of stuck to the news and I did feature, which is just covering stories and different events. And this year I'm Executive Editor so I had to switch to opinion. And as Executive Editor you like write for the school so like everything is like *"We as the Evanstonian feel. . ."* Which was kind of stressful at first, because like I don't know, it's just like hard thinking of an opinion the entire school would agree with. So I guess like this year it started with like the safety issue last year. And we wrote about how people need to respect safety, and like the attitude towards safety needs to change and like yes this one thing happened but we need to move past it. But I think that the biggest story that I've written about this year was one about sexual assault and it's because the original story was given to us by an ETHS student, she wanted her letter published and we were going to publish it instead of an editorial because we thought it fit better and was more appropriate than us re-writing the story. But the administration said that we couldn't, and I think that that was just a really hard thing for me because I'd always seen the administration as super helpful and willing to talk to you whenever, and this was the first time where they had threatened to like bring lawyers involved in like all the stuff and they were like, "*If you publish this, we're confiscating it.*" It was really just a hard thing to deal with. So we ended up rewriting the story, and I think that while it wasn't as beneficial as it could've been I think that telling her truth and her story through a way that could make the administration open their eyes, was really cool. And I remember like the Monday after meeting— like the Monday after issue came out, the teacher's Monday meeting was about sexual assault and my teacher said it was because of the editorial. And so it's cool to see an actual change that like a piece of my writing created.

The school that I went to North Carolina was private and everyone in North Carolina kind of went to private schools, it wasn't like a weird thing. Because like the public schooling system in North Carolina is like much worse than it is here. So like, coming to Evanston I was just kind of nervous. And then my brother actually hated Haven, like had to transfer out and he ended up at St. A's. But like I really liked Haven, I think that looking back on it there are a lot of— I was talking about this at lunch actually, there are so many flaws with like the school like now especially. I know that if you're like tardy to class, like even a minute they have like people sweeping the halls and you have to go to the auditorium instead of like going to class. And like the whole leggings scandal. . . and I think that there's just been a lot of scandals at Haven where you're just like, "*Why is this necessary?*" Because I remember it was like, it must've been like my first two weeks of school because I still didn't have a gym uniform yet. And I had gotten dressed coded, but it was like a male teacher and he was like— he like whispered to his assistant teacher "*You need to dress code her.*" And I remember being like, "*This is my mom's sweater. . . I don't have a gym uniform. . . I don't really know what you want me to do. . . Like I'm sorry but I actually have nothing else to wear.*" And she was like, "*You need to find a shirt.*" and I was like, "*OK. . .*" so I had to leave class and I like didn't go back, like I just couldn't find a shirt. I was new to the school I like literally didn't know people well enough to be like "*Hey guys. . .*" and like text people. . . so I think it's just like small things like that where they just really need to improve.

I've definitely seen prejudice and I think that taking Senior Studies has really opened my eyes to that prejudice. And I think like freshman, sophomore, junior year-what's the saying? "Ignorance is bliss"— and if like I don't know it or I don't recognize it it's not actually there. And I think that's kind of how I dealt with my problems, like you can ask Grace, I talked with her a lot about it and she be like, "*You're stupid, you're just not opening up your eyes to like all these things.*" and I'd be like, "*No but like it doesn't affect me.*" like all this stuff. But I think that this year I've kind of transitioned into like noticing it and trying to change it and I think that's largely attributed to Senior Studies for opening my eyes to it. I think that a major part of Evanston, like a major flaw in Evanston is that it's so falsely praised for being diverse, and while it may be diverse and numbers and statistics it's like not integrated at all. And it's like– everyone knows that ETHS is like two separate high schools. It's like rich, white northside kids come and like meet people who are just facing a very different Evanston. I think that one of the main problems is that no one really knows or experiences the other side of Evanston. And I think that like during the history unit, and stuff I've seen your studies, the biggest piece for me at least was like realizing and like being able to see the other side of Evanston and that's what helped me open my eyes more because there is like this other side that I'm just completely unfamiliar with. Even if it's just like volunteering at Park School, they're like living a completely separate Evanston than like what my experience is.

So, for my project I'm looking at three stigmatized issues in the media: race, sexual assault and mental disabilities. I'm doing a three piece of clothing collection to visually represent them and a three-piece journalism collection to verbally represent them. So, I'm printing out a four-page newspaper, so one page per article and then like an "All About Me" page kind of like saying why I feel like I have the right to write any of these articles in the first place. And like what my experience is and my background. Like how any of this pertains to me at all. And then like the clothing will be presented in an art gallery, and the clothing will be photographed inside the newspaper and so you'll be able to go through and read the article and then look at the clothes.

Nick Ingraffia

I'll start with my mom, my mom is from Allentown, Pennsylvania, she started working at Microsoft and so she moved to Chicago for that job she lived in like downtown near Lake Shore Drive for a second. My dad always lived in Chicago near like Wrigleyville. And I guess when he met my mom they lived together in Chicago and then they were like, "*Oh we're going to have kids so we're going to be boring middle-class, middle-aged white parents in Evanston, where all the middle-age white parents go.*"

So coming to high school was a super huge change because I'd always gone to a school that was like maybe 18 kids a grade. So like kindergarten to eighth grade I was with the same 18 kids, and coming to school that had almost 1000 kids a grade, was a huge transition, and freshman year I met so many people that I couldn't even keep track of how many people I met. I literally can't remember most of the people I met freshman year. It's been great so far, academically it's been fantastic, I've done fairly well academically, socially. . . not really. I try to get out of my bubble, like out of my small friend group and I do occasionally, but once you form like a tight friend group— like they seemed to solidify as the years go on. And so ETHS is generally segregated by friend groups, and like cliques, and also in like many other ways. . .

So Pope John was a very small and like closed and sheltered community that I was in. It's a private school and a Catholic school. We went to church like once a week, and we'd have religion class every single day. And you went to school and like if your shirt wasn't tucked in, if you chewed gum, if you had your nails painted or had any make-up on you either had to pay five dollars to the teacher that caught you or you got a demerit. And I actually got so many demerits in my last three years that I was supposed to be expelled. Because they're just like so ridiculous. Like just not tucking in your shirt or like not turning around your chair in class, like the teacher had full authority like it was like a dictatorship. And like if you even question a teacher, like if you question any authority at all, you got a demerit. But like the social scene— like it was really weird because it's like the same 18 kids for like the majority of my life, like nine years my life, like kindergarten through eighth grade. I'm not even 18 yet that was literally the majority of my life, at that school with the same 18 kids. And so, we got like really tight, we got to know who each person was like really, really well. So there was a lot of like positive energy because of that, but the positive energy was like super polarized and then the negative energy was also super polarized because of that. Like the kids who would get bullied, like we knew all about their families we knew like literally everything about their lives. And there was like a lot of bullying and like low-key racism because this is a really white school, like low-key racism, low-key homophobia and just like shaming of like most kids, like if you had a passion you would be shamed. Like I was terrified to have a passion outside of school work, like you'd be shamed, you'd be made fun of.

Evanston has definitely opened up my gender identity because before coming to ETHS, before coming to any LGBTQ community at all, like I didn't even question it. And I was a very flamboyant young kid and I was kind of bullied out of that. I was very much like, "*Oh yeah. That kid's the gay kid.*" *laughs* when I was a kid. And so I was bullied out of that and I kind of over emasculated myself, and there are still little trails of that now for sure. But then I was like exposed to the hugely— like even the facade of a welcoming community, I was like, "*Oh! Maybe I'm non-binary!*" And then the closet door creaks open and Nick Ingraffia jumps out.

Mainly in older Evanston and also in younger Evanston too but mainly an older Evanston, I always see like older white men— like recently I saw an older white man approach two young black females who were like playing music and just like looking at Snapchat stories. And he came up to them— no he didn't even come up to them! He reported them! He had the front office clerk come down and yell at them. And after the front desk man was politely like, "*Hey, can you guys like turn it down? Like this guy's not enjoying it.*" they were like, "*Okay yeah.*" and the guy just went off on them. Like the old man just went off on them and like yelled at them, "*You guys are so disrespectful, like you and your teens!*" And if those were like two white young girls, would he have yelled at them at all? Would he even have confronted them? And there's so many more examples I'm skipping on, but like even my parents, like my parents are super prejudiced, they're not racist in the sense that they believe that their race is higher than other races but like they're definitely prejudice and have like a very traditional mindset. Like my mom recently has been reading these environmentalist books and watched like Moonlight and heard a bunch of things about Donald Trump and she's like, "*Oh this is so horrible what is happening in our country, it's terrible like I'm looking back at what happened with like Christopher Columbus and I am so ashamed of what my race has done.*" And I'm like, "*Yes mom.*" And then she's like, "*Sometimes I think America isn't as great as I thought it was.*" And she always has had this like really traditional mindset, and I think it's the same with like a lot of Evanston. Like it's becoming trendy to be socially conscious but when it comes down to the core of like who you are and how you were raised and how you actually believe how prejudice affects your life, nothing really has changed. But like it also has helped with politics, like a liberal movement, like even if it's like a pseudo-liberal, like a fake liberal movement, like in politics like if it looks cool to like pass liberal and like progressive policies, politicians are going to do that, so go ahead, doesn't matter how we get there, but do it please!

I want to see more trees in Evanston. Definitely more trees. . . free the beaches. And I want like natural beaches. I also want like more venues, and a bigger art scene, and they're already kind of is but it's more DIY and it needs to be more established. More. . . self-sustainability because we kind of leech off Chicago for like almost everything— like I'm talking about culture wise and job-wise, I hate like this suburb feeling of like, *"Everyone lives here but it's like a super transient place 'cause everyone just goes down to Chicago for like everything."* Like everyone goes down to the marches in Chicago but like. . . why don't we just have marches here? Like there should be a lot more organization amongst the Evanston community instead of like gravitating toward Chicago. Because no one takes initiative here, or like in that sense, because we can just hop on the backs of Chicago.

So for my project I'm writing a book, and exploring how I best express myself, through writing but the farther I go along I get, the farther and farther away from not writing— I just want to branch off into like different ways to express myself. And I'm studying how the writing process goes and how I can personalize that within myself and like how that happens on a professional level. And just how a book gets published. It sounds really pretentious– but my book is about, it's about the relationship between the mind and body, how the world around it affects it and how it affects the world around it. And it is told through a story about a teenager who first separates themselves mentally from society, then separates themselves physically from society, then separates themselves physically from the world. And then mentally separates from their physical self.

Jaylyn Jimenez

Okay, so high school for me started off I guess like anybody else. I think this happens to most people, but my friend group kind of fell apart, and all my friends from middle school were like white and I don't know I never really thought about it. I wasn't in TWI, I didn't like go to a TWI elementary school— sorry I'm like going really far back, but I went to Lincoln and there wasn't a lot of Latinos there. And so then, when I went to Nichols I wasn't in like the TWI Spanish program, so even though I'm like fluent in Spanish I had to take like Spanish 1 and Spanish 2 and like I asked— and now I'm in a native speaker class, but in middle school I wasn't, and I always asked the teachers like, "*Can I please be in the TWI class?*" or it was called

Spanish Heritage in middle school, so, *"Can I please be in Span-ish Heritage?"* And they be like, *"No because you help us teach the classes."* Yeah. Like both of my teachers each year told me that since I helped the other students I couldn't leave. It was such B.S. and I f***ing hated it. And so it sucked, like I had to learn vocabulary, like the ABCs and like it just sucked, it was horrible. And like I never got to connect with like the Latinos at my school because they kept me separated because I didn't come from a TWI school. And they looked at me like I was different because they were all kept together and I like wasn't with them. And I don't know, it just really sucked.

And so, when I went to high school something that I really liked was being able to connect with the other Latinos in Evanston be-cause I got to test out of like the regular Spanish class, like I was in Spanish 2 when I came, and the teacher was like, *"Wait. . . this isn't for you."* So, then I tested out of it and I got to be in Heritage, and I like finally met all the Latinos from the other schools, and I like recon-nected with the ones from Nichols and it was just like so much bet-ter. Not because I don't like white people, just like before. . . I don't know, before I felt like I wasn't Hispanic enough for Evanston. But I wasn't like white enough for Evanston. . . And I'm not black— like I don't consider myself African American, so I was just like a floater, like I didn't know where it belonged. And like all my friends were white— just like the cultural differences sometimes would make me feel like an outsider. So my favorite part of high school is definitely the opportunities I've had to connect with other Latino students and Latino teachers. And I don't know it just made me find out a lot more about myself and my culture, and it's just been like an awesome ex-perience. Like summits and like staying after classes. . .

But like some negative aspects– like some of the teachers were just so rude, like some of my teachers I do feel like treated me dif-ferently because they know I'm Latina and my family's Latino. And like they treated me really rudely because like they think— like they assume that my parents like don't speak English or like my parents aren't going to come fight for me like a white kid's parents would. And so that has been like really hard because it just makes me feel like they think that me and my family– like they think my parents don't care about me, cause I think they wouldn't treat me like that if they thought that I had parents who cared enough to say something. But then I don't have my parents say something because I don't want the teacher to treat me even worse. It's just like a vicious cycle. And then, kind of feeling like ETHS definitely caters to white people. I just feel like ETHS doesn't make much of an effort to like do outreach– I don't know, it's hard to make a statement because whenever I'm like, "*ETHS just doesn't do this. . .*" I think of something that they do, you know what I mean? Like other schools aren't having like summits, other schools wouldn't give like brown kids, like me, resources like the ones ETHS does have. There are some schools where there are no Latino teachers, there are no black teachers, and I could be there but I'm not, so, you know what I'm trying to say? They make an effort, it's just not cutting it.

I've always felt like at ETHS if you're not white or black you're just not there. Like that's how I've been treated and I feel like Latinos have been treated in high school. And in ETHS, in general—definitely caters to white people with like AP classes and like honors classes, and definitely in the way that teachers and administration go about things, like I said, they're so rude and mean to like people of color because they think that their parents don't care. And like they're not going to like throw a fit and like write a letter, and I feel like a lot of white parents do, you know? Like I just feel like they pick on us for everything, and I'm not trying to sound like a little kid like, "*They're picking on us!*" but like it's true. From like detention to like dress code, in class interaction. . . just like the way brown kids are treated from the way white kids are treated is just like so different, and yeah it's just really frustrating.

So I have another example of one of those "teachers being mean and thinking that my parents don't care" things— and my parents actually didn't say anything because I told them not to because I was afraid of how the teacher would treat me. In like freshman year, it was in like geometry— and I'm like horrible at math, like I've barely passed every year of math and I was going in for extra help, because like I said, again, I did not get it, I just could not understand. So, just like any good student I was there in the morning to get help and like every time, he would just give me practice problems, but I didn't know how to do them so like I would just sit there and felt really awkward because I was like embarrassed about the fact that I didn't know how to do them. And since they were practice problems I felt like, "*Oh these are supposed to be helping me and I don't even know how to do it, like this is probably the simplest thing and I still don't know how to do it.*" So anyway after like the third time I came in and he had given me like practice problems and I was like, "*I don't know what to do with this. . . I don't know how to do it.*" And he was like, "*Yeah Jaylyn, I could give you a $20 bill and you would still tell me you don't know how to use it, you don't know what to do with it because you don't know what to do with anything I give you in my class.*" And I like wanted to cry. And it was like so so embarrassing, like one of the most embarrassing moments of my life. And obviously my parents were like so upset, and I told them not to do anything (which I regret) I just thought that, "*If this is how he treats me now what is he going to do if my parents– like how is he going to treat me if he already feels comfortable treating me like this?*"

It was just frustrating because I would see like white kids from his higher-level classes come in for extra help or questions and he be so eager to help them, like so glad that they're like advocating for their education. But like when I came in, like a freshman and one of his lower level classes, who is trying to learn, comes in for help I'm all of a sudden like annoying him. And like "*I'm not trying. . .*" and stuff like that. But like how much more can I try, I'm like coming in in the morning for help like I don't get it. And like that's the experience for a lot of brown kids in Evanston. And this is a little bit unrelated but I was talking to this adult who speaks Spanish and she's Latina and she volunteers in classrooms as a translator for conferences and stuff. And like sometime she'll be sitting there with a student's parents and the teacher. . . she said that the teachers will sometimes be like, "*All the other white kids will come in and like advocate for themselves but like the Latino kids never do and I just like wonder why. Like why aren't they coming in in like advocating for themselves? And like asking questions?*" Because like we know that's what you think about us, like that you think that we don't care about our education anyways.

And then also like, Dean Bumbry, freshman year— me and some friends were basically jumped outside of the school, after football game. Like right after football game we were walking to Annie Doyle's house and she lives right across the street from Cherry Preschool, so pretty close to ETHS, and we were on the corner of Dodge like right by the sign and we are crossing the street and like these boys like grabbed my butt so I turned around and I was like, *"What the f***! Like can you not do that."* But like louder and like more upset. And like long story short they like kept on crossing the street, like getting towards where we were and like harassing us and like trying to grab us and like take us with them, and then they were trying to follow us and like chasing us around and like touching us. . . it was horrible. And we had to report it to Dean Bumbry and she was just like so rude about it the entire time and told us that we should've like— she was like, *"You should've crossed the street as soon as you saw them. I don't care if it's racial profiling."* Like we had to tell her what they looked like and they were black. And she was like, *"I don't care if it's racially profiling you should cross the street, you should've been walking with your keys in your hand."* And like all of the stupid s***. And I was kind of asking her like, *"What are you gonna do about it?"* And she was kind of asking like, *"What do you expect us to do?"* And it was really scary and I kept on telling her like, *"No one was there and it was at the corner of the school, like right by the field. . . like right by this big sign that says ETHS, you would figure that there'd be security there."* And I was like, *"No one was there, no one was there."* And she's like, *"What do you expect ETHS to have 24 seven security?"* And was just like super condescending and like, *"You should've been aware of your surroundings."* Like literally we were crossing the street, they were crossing the street right after football game literally right outside of our school, in our town, like how more aware of our surroundings could we be?

I talk a lot about issues I have with ETHS, but I feel like because I do that people think that I hate Evanston, and I don't. Like I love Evanston, like I love the fact that grown up in Evanston I think it's like beautiful and I like the people I've met here. I personally live in like South Evanston so I live really close to downtown, really close Rogers Park. And I really like that I'm really close to that. And obviously, like I got a lot from the Evanston school systems, like all the great things that Evanston has to offer, I really love that about Evanston. And just the culture here— even though it's frustrating that Evanston can be like an echo chamber, like everyone likes to claim that they're so "woke" and liberal and non-racist, it's nice to live in a place where like that's what you have to do to fit in. Instead of it being like, *"Oh to fit in you have to be like an a**hole to everyone and be racist."* Even though some people are fake I'd rather live somewhere where the norm is acceptance, you know?

But I think that living here has made me even more proud to be Latina. It's made me extremely comfortable with like standing out, I like standing out, I like to speak out and that's a big part of my iden- tity— like always having something to say. And like I always volun- teer myself to speak and give my opinion, and I think Evanston has really shaped that more because I always feel like people want me to shut up either because I'm a girl or because I'm Latina or because I'm brown or whatever. So it just like pushed me even more. And of course it's like made me really liberal and accepting.

I would like people here to stop being so afraid of what they re- ally think, you know? And like back up their own statements and not like have to write an anonymous letter about like Curt's Café's Black Lives Matter sign in their window, or like hide behind Facebook posts in like our school page. Like Curts Café had like a Black Lives Matter sign and like this guy wrote like this huge letter about how they need to take down that sign and how like the Black Lives Mat- ter movement is a whole bunch of criminals and it's a lie. . . and like it's not true, like he said that in the letter he was like, *"You need to take that down because it's not true."* And he was basically just say- ing "All Lives Matter" and s*** like that and he signed it Andrew…? What the f***, no one knows who you are Andrew. I feel like– it's great that Evanston's liberal, I really like that but I feel like we're also really quick to be like, *"That's racist that's racist! That's Transphobic! That's that!"* And yet it's good that we call it out but we're literally making people so afraid of being judged because they're not like the liberal-ist. Like I'll admit I don't know a lot of stuff about like gender stuff and I like mess up all the time and like say things that I later learned are like so offensive. Not because of like slurs or anything, but like for a while I was like, "*I don't get how like signs at like Women's Marches with uteruses, like stuff like that— I don't get how that's like Trans Exclusionary Feminism? Sorry but like I have a uterus and this is what I'm talking about.*" And like I didn't understand how like that's like so f***ed up, like I didn't understand– like that I was like a Trans Exclusionary Feminist! Like I didn't realize it! And I just wish that more people in Evanston felt comfortable enough to be like, "*Hey I don't agree.*" But we're also open minded enough to have that discussion, because I would've stayed like that. But I thought that people were just being like super sensitive and like touchy, like I felt like offended!

Okay so my project is a social media campaign to educate people and kind of change the way people see Latinos in Evanston, in Chicago and Latino neighborhoods in Chicago by showing different positive aspects of our culture, like art, food music and like storytelling. . . so, yeah.

Ryan Johnson

So, my mom was born in Evanston, Illinois and dad was born on the southside of Chicago, Englewood. They both went to Southern Illinois University Carbondale, which is a couple hours from here and. . . they met in college. My mom was, I wasn't really too sure what her major was, but I know she wanted to go into the fashion industry, she loved like, designing. And then my dad was completely different and then they met at a party or whatever, like a college party. And my mother she had actually pledged Alpha Kappa Alpha sorority incorporated, graduate chapter instead of in her college year because she said something was going on there and she wasn't really thinking about a sorority. And then they kind of moved up here. . . He fell in love with her and he would go wherever she went, so they came back to Evanston.

So, in high school I guess— I liked it a lot: I learned how to balance and use my time wisely. I definitely have encountered some negatives in high school, I would say maybe with like finding the right groups to be around and making new friends and coming from a really small elementary and middle school: Bessie Rhodes Magnet School. It was like forty 8th graders and you know, if you didn't fit in with the five cliques there, you didn't really have a group and you didn't really have friends. And that was kinda me. But coming to high school— coming to ETHS I really enjoyed talking with people, like getting to know different backgrounds and cultures and I would definitely say that's a highlight of my high school career. And, you know, I feel like I've definitely been prepared for college and gotten ready to like, go on to bigger things and start a new beginning and it's definitely prepared me a lot. So I think my positives have definitely outweighed my negatives.

I had some likes and dislikes of Bessie Rhodes. With it being such a small school when we ate lunch in the cafeteria we had to eat with the kindergarteners and first graders, we were all cramped in one space. We didn't have locker rooms. It was just very interesting how small it was. . . but I feel that— going to that school, I've definitely met a lot of people, like where they were at one point my best friend or they were people I really gained close relationships with. I think I also really enjoyed it because the education and teaching skills the teachers gave us, and the curriculum was very intriguing and it definitely made me think like, "Oh, I will really need this in high school." or "I could definitely use this in my career." And a lot of things I know now, I think if I didn't go to Bessie Rhodes, I wouldn't really be too familiar with. I would definitely say that Bessie Rhodes, with it being so small— it was really small but it was really empowering too as well because I gained close relationships with teachers and the faculty and staff and were always really helpful and always wanted to make me push myself more and not really, you know, think of ways to put myself down or if I didn't complete something just think "Oh I'll *never get it done."*— I never thought negative when I went to that school. So I really enjoyed it— yeah.

I definitely have experienced prejudice in Evanston, I would say there have been times where I have been walking in Downtown Evanston with a group of friends and maybe, mind you, it would just be two or three of my friends and of course we are, African American, and we would walk into a store, like Urban Outfitters or American Apparel and— with that store kind of being majority white workers it would definitely make us feel uncomfortable. We would get looked at funny, to make sure we weren't stealing or like we would always think to ourselves like, *"Oh they probably think we won't be able to buy this because it's too expensive."* or you know. . . So we kind of really thought about whether or not we would feel welcome in that area or that space and if it was mainly for one race or just for white people so, that was one thing we definitely did encounter. So it kind of made us feel some type of way, of just being looked at like, *"Oh well we know black people steal."* or like maybe that, *"Black girls want this, this, and this, but it's like, your money is funny."* or *"You don't know how to balance paying for this, this, and this."* So I thought it was very interesting and it was shocking to think that we would still live in an era where there is this much prejudice but a lot of times I would just not let it affect me because I know what I am capable of doing and it wouldn't matter of anyone else's opinion is.

I think that with going to ETHS, I am more confident with myself being a black woman. And that me going to a diverse school, that I'm very, very comfortable with people outside of my race I can, you know, definitely connect with, or have a conversation with. I've never been like too hesitant to talk about anything and I think it's definitely motivated me to push and actually empower future generations or people who don't have that confidence or like have that growth to actually build and push up for themselves.

I think a change I would like to see is maybe. . . more African Americans pushing up others— and other minorities. Since we are labeled as the minority, a lot of people think that like, they— the minority specifically isn't capable of doing certain things, such as, you know, for example: taking AP classes, or just taking different courses that are challenging that you wouldn't expect someone of a minority to take. I think like pushing each other up and telling each other like, "*You can do it!*" and actually like, being that figure of just, empowerment. That's really important and should happen more in Evanston, and definitely just telling people like, "*I am right with you, I'm struggling too. We can struggle together, to meet each other's needs and kind of, push for where we want to go.*"

I decided to focus my project on microaggressions and stereotypes of African American teenage girls in the Evanston and Chicago communities. I really thought about this topic, my junior research paper was on a similar topic as such, it was on finding the confidence levels of a black woman and a white woman. I've always just had a passion for talking about, specifically my race and how I connect to so many other girls who are of African descent. I think that the stereotypes of black women— they're always negative and it's never pinpointed of what African American women have done successfully. African American women have been motivators, instructors, you know, just like wonderful women that want to help generations, and us young girls and build up and boost our confidence levels. So, I think that it was very important to talk about this and I feel like with my survey that I conducted and the questions I asked that I would get a lot of responses from Evanston and Chicago. And comparing both schools I can definitely see where most of the stereotypes and microaggressions happened and hopefully sometime in our society or maybe later on in the years, the negative stereotypes and negative connotations can be put to a halt because, I personally, think that that's not every African American girl so there shouldn't be one label on us and I don't think we such be targeted for what people would classify us as or what we represent. So, I just have always had a passion for this, like I said and I think that it's very important that we talk about this, and we educate people on things that they don't know about. . . or stereotypes that they don't really know but say about us African Americans, as a whole.

Oliver Kamholtz-Roberts

Okay— I'm creating a podcast, basically about what it means to be trans at ETHS. The first— well I've only been working on the first episode so far, but that one's dealing with the lack of policy that we have surrounding what facilities trans students can use. So what I'm trying to highlight is just the confusion and the difference between how the administration is thinking about it and how students are experiencing it. Right now there is no official policy, because we don't yet have the laws to back it up, so we can't, um— there are just procedures in place but there isn't official policies that are really protecting trans students by law. And. . . so, there's "Locker Room Three", which is just a third locker room, it's very small, um, all trans students regardless of their gender identity are expected to change in there. As of— this actually just happened recently, that trans students are now allowed to use the bathroom that corresponds with whatever their identity is. A few months ago we were told that we just had to use the gender neutral bathroom, of which there are like three maybe. But in the last few weeks they've actually said, "*Okay, you can go in whatever bathroom you want.*" But the locker rooms are still like, the big question, that um, it seems there aren't enough conversations happening about.. . . So, I've been interviewing fellow trans students and then also administrators, just to try to highlight like the difference in— in how administrators think what is happening and trans students are experiencing it— so Ms. Patterson, Dr. Campbell....

I feel like my experience of ETHS is very like— it's a very small part of the whole of ETHS, cause I like basically just exist in the theater department, but I adore it. I spend a lot of my time in the Upstairs Theater. It's a very like— I feel weird trying to equate it to all of ETHS because it's a very, like, isolated community, but I love the theater community. It's very— very queer! And, um, yeah it was just— it's like a very open community. Mr. Herbert and Mr. Carney, who direct and teach the department, feel like parents to me, so I feel very like connected in my part of the Evanston community. And of course it was like a— literally a perfect place for me to like come out and be comfortable and chill. Yeah, I think I have like very little interaction with like the rest of ETHS.

I really love Senior Studies! I basically— I think all of us basically had no say in where our education was going until second semester senior year and so that's obviously my favorite part about it, is just being able to decide what I'm doing and choose to study things that I care about. And then needless to say also, all 74 of us are. . . I feel like there's a dynamic there that you don't get in a lot of other classes. A very close. . . a closeness that I don't find at all, outside of the theater department at ETHS.

I feel like there's a lot of gender stuff that I could talk about, so I just want to get that out of the way so I can actually talk about other stuff, as well! Evanston obviously— my circles in Evanston have been more than accepting and very like— like I don't think I would have realized I was trans if I lived somewhere that was more conservative or enforcing of gender roles, maybe. Aside from that though, I feel like Evanston allowed me to be like, weird. I feel like, I've talked to a lot of people who after high school went to college somewhere else and were like, *"Oh, I can be, like, weird."* Um, and I think that like from 6th grade people in Evanston— people I know in Evanston have felt able to just be like, weird. However, I do feel like Evanston is— I feel like we all do a lot of talking about how perfect Evanston is. And part of Senior Studies, the first semester was kind of uncovering. . . the vast imperfections of Evanston, and so many problems that we still have— especially like self-segregation and class issues and just like separation of parts of Evanston and just like lack of communication. . . and actual equality. Yeah, I don't think Evanston's perfect by any stretch, and Senior Studies made me more aware of that.

I'd like to see Evanston change. . . probably the idea that it's perfect, I feel like if people stopped believing that Evanston is like this haven of integration and happiness— and like, I think if we stopped believing that it's perfect, we'd want to do more to change it. I think people are clinging really strongly to this idea of like, *"Evanston is so far ahead of other communities, so we have no work to do."*

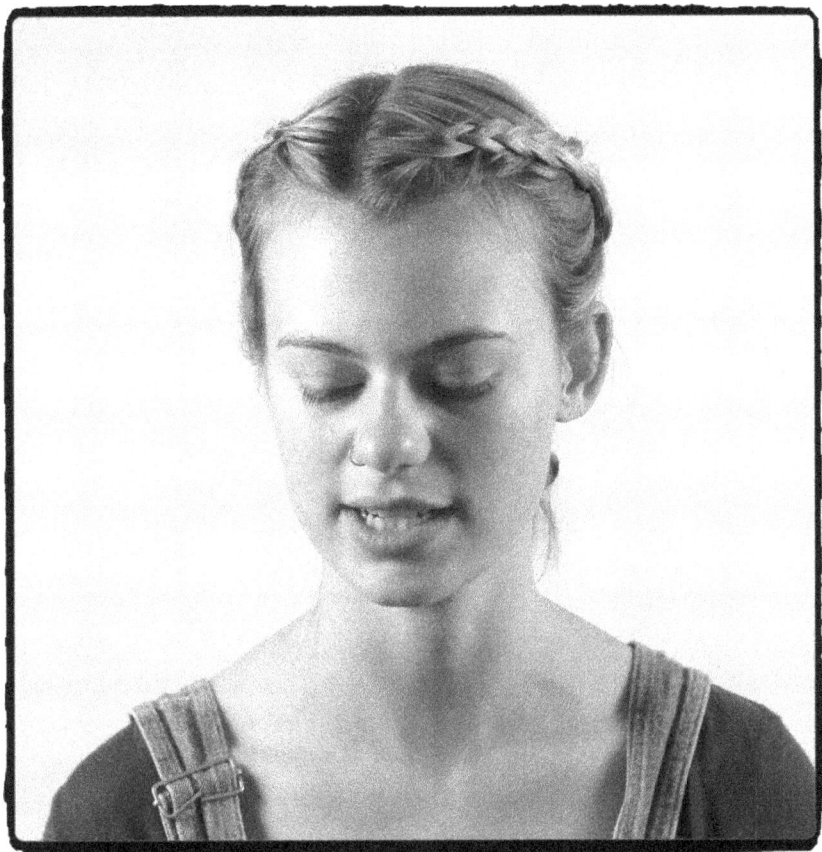

Cecilia **Kearney**

So my dad and my stepmom were born in Wilmette– born and raised in Wilmette. And they've actually known each other since preschool, and then they went separately for college. And like got back together after college. And yeah so they grew up in Wilmette, and my dad had a really horrible experience there– he hated it. Okay so he just read so much and he's always read a bunch, and he was very aware of the apartheid that basically Wilmette is and just how much of a bubble it was just in terms of like how nobody really cared about what was going on outside of Wilmette. And so he would like stay home from school and like read all these books, like these philosophy books and history books. And so he decided basically that he was not going to raise his kids in Wilmette, like he was going to move out after high school, and he did. Now we live in Evanston, which is like *laughs* a step better. And my stepmom had a decent time, like she had a good childhood. She went to Northwestern so she stayed around here and discovered that she liked Evanston a lot better.

I think for me every year of high school has gotten better, socially. I've definitely cycled through different friend groups, and I've had like one consistent friend since like sixth grade, Jazmin, which is been really good. Definitely getting involved with clubs has helped, like feel more involved. . . like with DREAMERS club. I don't know I think Evanston Township High School is a good high school but I think going anywhere is going to be hard at this time in your life. And I didn't realize that as much until I'm kind of growing out of it now.

So I was in TWI, I went to Washington and I loved it, I absolutely adored it and I didn't realize it until this year/last year that it was not the same experience for everyone. Half the class for TWI is kids who grew up speaking Spanish, most of them immigrated from Mexico or Guatemala, and they had a very different experience. Talking to them now, and like realizing how much of the system— the TWI system was designed for white kids, to benefit white kids. Like it's supposed to be to benefit both and everyone learns Spanish, everyone learns English. But it's a lot of like, "Oh white kids you get to have cultural immersion." And like, "You got to have this amazing experience." And with the Latino kids I felt like the focus was definitely not on them as much. And definitely after fifth grade when we went to middle school there was more of a divide, we didn't have classes together, we only had Spanish class together. And like we stopped hanging out together, it was weird and I wish I had done more to make an effort to stop that. To keep up connections with people, because we used to like, go to each other's houses, like have birthday parties together, but the community just kind of like fell apart. Partially because I was in one of the first years that they did it and they didn't really have a plan for what was going to happen in middle school. But I think parents and kids definitely could've taken initiative. It's gotten a little better, there still working it out though. My siblings are in TWI right now, it's interesting they are more African-

American kids in TWI now, there were none when I was there. There was always a weird divide between Gen Ed and TWI. The white kids and the black kids were in Gen Ed, and in some ways the more educated white kids were in TWI— it was weird we like didn't mix a lot.

I think for TWI, I would definitely like to see the integration continue, in middle school and it just like stopped abruptly after fifth grade. I would like teachers and parents to facilitate that more because six graders are kind of clueless in a lot of ways, and I think that can definitely be done a lot better, and I think people are working on that now. Also— I don't know I've been thinking a lot about gentrification lately, it's definitely evident. . . like Peckish Pig on Howard Street. Like when you walk in it's just this like weird little white dot on Howard Street. I've researched it and people who live on the block or whatever have talked about how it's like— it's cool and it like increases their property value, which isn't necessarily a good thing, but some people are like "*My property have gone up in value!*" But they're like, "*I don't feel welcome there.*" like they're like, "*It's so clearly not made for me.*" And also around the high school like there's more buildings like being renovated, and apartments being renovated with nicer kitchens, and the rent is going up. I have friends who live around here and their parents are like struggling to pay rent because everything is being renovated and like being priced for so much higher. And it's harder to have access to this because the schools are so good and so the property taxes go up. . . and so it's weird, it's like complicated. And I would like to see more restaurants and cafés like Curt's Cafe, like they're there and they improve the community, but they also give back to people in the community, and help and it's accessible for people there.

I've definitely seen other people experience prejudice, my best friends since sixth grade is from Belize and she's always had– just like seeing her become more comfortable with her identity and hearing her talk about how she's assimilated to like white culture, and like had white friends– mostly white friends, all the s*** she's gone through is just insane because we've been friends for so long but she's just experienced such a different world. And it's so different— our experiences are just incredibly different. And I think definitely is a female I've experienced prejudice but it's nothing compared to a person of color. But yeah definitely small backhanded comments from teachers to students of color, a lot. Parents being weirded out by their kids bringing home people of color. . . definitely seen that.

So my project is advocating and raising money for DREAMERS club and trying to raise awareness in the Evanston community about the immigrant and undocumented community in Evanston. Two of my best friends are undocumented and through them I've got to see how the college process is different and how it's way more difficult, it's a difficult to begin with, but it's like so much more difficult for undocumented students who can't get federal or financial aid. And DREAMERS club is a scholarship that goes to undocumented students, and so I had a community art event where people came in and did art, bought art and looked at art. . . and all the money went to the scholarship. We raised almost $1000. The scholarship is only two years old, and the first year it was like $2000, and then last year (the second year) it was $3000 or something. . . and we already have like $5000 this year so it's just like increasing. . . And it's gonna get so much bigger as time passes and they become more established.

Maddie Lee

My mom was born in Evanston, and grew up here. My dad— I don't know where he was born. . . Atlanta maybe? I don't know he moved around a lot cuz his dad was in the military. But he ended up here because he was living in Chicago and he met my mom, cuz they were both volunteering at a hospital. And she was from Evanston, so they both moved here when they were like getting serious.

So overall freshman, sophomore year— super great school years. Happy place. Um and then junior year, like when the sexual assault happened, it was like once I tried to get the help that I needed I wasn't really able to get that, cuz I wasn't able to report it. I'm not really sure of the policies, I just know that I was talking to the social worker about it and my specific social worker was great, but just because the nature of the crime, I guess. . . And she like asked specifically like she was like, "*Did you have any bruises? Like do you have pictures bruises?*" And like cuz I didn't I wasn't able to do anything about it, so, that was hard administration-wise. Just like not super receiving the support that I needed. And just like the building feeling a lot less safe with him in it, I guess? So junior year was really hard, and then when he left— I mean, senior year is great. It's just nice to know how many good people are in the building, and like getting that safety back.

My experience in Evanston. . . I mean it definitely feels like home, I dunno. I think Evanston has made me very much the person that I am— (I think) someone who cares a lot about people around them and. . . I dunno, wants a community and also wants to support people, who are possibly less privileged than I am, in anyway that I can. I think growing up in a place that has so many differences and also like— but wanting to pretend that everything is positive, you know, it's like when you're younger it's like, "*Evanston's great! Look at all this diversity!*" and then when you get older it's like, "*Oh Evanston's still great. . . but like. . . yikes!*" you know? Or like realizing there's a lot of stuff you just didn't know, it was kind of like— like taking the veil of your head. And then realizing that some people didn't even get to live with that veil at all. In general, I think it's a community that tries, I guess, I mean maybe not historically. . . but it tries.

I'd like to see more— more honesty, I think. I think just like— I mean all the things that everyone wants, like integration and less economic disparities. But I think just being more honest about that and not pretending that this is like some sort of sanctuary and we have no problems. . . I guess.

So, I'm doing a circus routine but the music to the routine is going to be a poem about strong womanhood. So there's going to be, probably around 4 women on stage reading their part of the poem that they wrote and then one woman performing the routine. So it's going to be like, different ways to tell the many different ways that women are women. Like to demonstrate strong womanhood. So at the presentations I'm doing my talk— well I'm kind of still figuring it out, but I'm doing like my talk about what I did all semester, and then I'm going to do the routine. So I can show people what I made. And then I'm hopefully going to have like little stand for like different places that support women, that they can donate to, like Planned Parenthood, or the YWCA (where I work) and places like that.

Olivia **Lemmenes**

My parents. . . I think my mom was born here in Evanston and my dad. . . I think was born in Wisconsin, and his parents are from the Netherlands. I'm not totally sure if they were like the first immigrants and their family to come over, maybe second. My mom, she's like a whole mixture of white (cause I'm adopted) she's a whole mixture of like different European ethnicities. . . My mom— since she's lived in Evanston for all of her life, she loved it here, and when my dad met her I think they chose the Evanston/Chicago area because they just like really liked it.

I think ETHS has been interesting. . . definitely freshman, sopho-more year I cared a lot about my appearance I guess and the way

I acted around certain people, like the "popular people" and like when I'd be around them I get kinda like nervous and I think like, "*Oh I need to present myself in like a certain way*". And then like junior year and senior year I realized that like that doesn't matter, and there isn't like any "popular people", it was pretty much all in my head. . . And I learned to just be myself around anyone, and just not like. . . focus on what I wear to school, what I say or stuff like that.

I went to Bessie Rhodes so I knew the graduating class since like kindergarten – like the majority of them. And it was interesting growing up with them because like you could see how they changed. I think it's also interesting because (since I'm adopted) when I was younger I was super excited and like I wanted to share with people, like who I was and like my ethnicity and stuff. Like I thought it was cool to be adopted and stuff like that, and then like throughout like fourth grade through like maybe middle school I wasn't as proud as that, and like I tried to hide it, I think as much as I could. Even at like the beginning of high school I was kind of like, "*Ehh I'm adopted and I have white parents and like most my friends are white.*" and stuff like that, and just kind of like hiding the fact that I was Chinese, and stuff like that. Because I remember when I was younger, in like elementary school I would always like during Chinese New Year, I would always bring treats and stuff from Chinatown and explain to the class about like Chinese New Year and what it means and what they do in China. And as I got older that excitement kind of faded, and I think now it's coming back and I'm really happy about it. And I think that District 65— I don't know if it was the people that I hung out with or if it was just like me growing up and trying to figure out who I was. . . I think that that was a big part of my life though.

My mom specifically forced me to do like Chinese school, and I rebelled the lot, especially during that time when I was like, "*No, I don't want to be a part of it.*" And when I was younger my mom and my dad would try to go to Chinese school with me, and learn Chinese. And they tried as much as they could to like be a part of that culture, as I'm a part of this culture.

I think us talking about (in Senior Studies this year) about the bussing that happens in Evanston really opened my eyes because I, as like an elementary student I didn't really notice this, like it didn't really occur to me that like most of the black students were getting on the bus, or like the students of color in general were getting on the bus. I mean I wouldn't be bused home I would go— my mom just pick me up but I mean my house is like 10/15 minutes away. So that was interesting learning about that and hearing about that, because I guess I didn't know too much about that at the beginning of the year.

Honestly, I think in general Evanston is really. . . well rounded, I think. We have a lot of resources, and I guess a change I would like to see, this is a weird way to put it, but like better advertising of these resources. Like there's so many different resources that I'm thinking of just off of my Senior Studies project, I was looking at mental health resources around Evanston and there are so many and I didn't know about like most of these. And like there are specific resources that are like affordable, and I think in general we have so many resources that we take advantage of most of them and like most people don't know about them, I think. I mean probably a lot of people do because like they're still up and going, but like I feel like there's just a lot of resources here that people don't know about. . .

So, I am working to destigmatize mental health, specifically depression in teenagers. I would like to create a book with student submissions from ETHS or honestly any school, about how people have experienced depression, and either how they've gotten through it or advice or whatever they want to give and share to their audience. And this is all gonna be anonymous. And I'm also putting my own writing and resources around Evanston in the book. And it's not gonna be a big book— maybe 20 to 30 pages. But then I'm also working on a resource sheet that I'm hopefully going to put around Evanston Township High School and I want this resource sheet to be more appealing, and give students easy access to resources because I feel like right now students either have to go through social workers or, or teachers or counselors and ask for a list of resources around Evanston. And I feel like as a teenager if you're struggling with mental illness, I feel like that's not who you want to go to, you don't want to go to a counselor that you might not like, or a teacher that you have for one year or social worker who you don't know who they are. I just want students to have better access to these resources. So I'm working with the school and we're going to either put a link to the social work page on the ETHS website or a link to the resource sheet that I made on the website, so students can access it really easily.

Jack Lickerman

A very positive experience I've had here has been. . . I guess when I go other places— when I have gone other places, for example when I went to jazz camp this summer I felt an absence in my life and it took me a while to realize what that was, and it was because there were only white people there. And while maybe all of my close friends are white, just— I see a bunch of different kinds of people every single day walking around Evanston and ETHS, so thats a huge privilege, for sure, just it being an integrated community. I think the music program here is amazing and I've had— it's like infinite resources— like I've learned so much, I've had so much to learn from the music program. And I think public school is an extremely important asset, especially going to a public school like ETHS, where it's kinda like— it's like so cushy and so nice, but then also compared to like North Shore Country Day and like the French school my brother goes— my younger brother goes, in Winnetka, and it costs $16,000 a year for preschool, so yeah, that kind of thing and the track that he's gonna go on, it's like super cushy. And ETHS is super cushy, but it is kind of— like it hardens you like you have to interact with people and push your way through stuff— I don't know that kind of sounds like "Boot Strap Theory" but I kind of feel like you need to be an independent person in general and the high school being such a free for all, makes you be that way, like you have to go defend your education and you have to go to the teachers and like go talk to people if you wanna make stuff happen. A negative experience would be just the overall— I mean it's going away now because people are like getting afraid and because it's so trendy to be critical of liberal culture, but like something that is just upsetting and bad in Evanston is the overall idea that like— like post racial type stuff, just excusing the possibility of like the notion of an issue at its conception. Like before you even start to think— like *"Oh there's no possible way it could exist."* Just like not acknowledging an issue and pretending that a sign in your front yard or like *"not seeing color"* or some s*** like that, addresses it. Like I think there's a lot of people here that cause regression and like stop change because they don't want to actually do anything, there's a lot of people who just want to talk about stuff. I dunno just like the trendiness of activism and stuff, like I think it's good, but….

District 65 was awesome, also another public school— I'm a super advocate for public school because being in a big environment, I mean if you can't handle it that's okay but it makes you more independent. What was my experience like? Good, for the most part. Something, you know, that is true to all primary education in America is that like there's— I remember, I mean I feel like the genocide of indigenous peoples and like slavery, I feel like it was just like a sentence, like the more I think back it was like *"this happened and that happened."* Like I feel like I could reduce my comprehensive history, of non-white history of America into like a sentence, from District 65. So I would say that would be a negative thing, but a positive thing. . . I was in an integrated environment before racialized conditioning and prejudice started converting who I spoke with and who I hang out with now, you know, 'cause it still does. Like before there was this *"You hang out with this kind of people"*, I hung out with a lot of different people who don't live anywhere near me, and that was cool, like getting to see *"Oh those people don't walk the same way I do, why is that?"* getting to be in a different environment— integrated environment, socioeconomically.

This year there was this referendum— I know it's a proposition that will raise everyone's property taxes $39 a month which. . . I dunno I wish there was a way that was like, *"$160,000 a year plus, you have to pay it."* There's just no easy way to go about doing it because you could have five kids and make that much money and it's spread really tight. Like, I think it's good and I'm totally in support of it, but something I felt like— Mr. Jhunjhunwala actually made me think about was like, I was like, *"Yeah that band, we're dope like we're coming in full force and we marched—"* I didn't actually see it, did you see it, like on the news? Well, Maya organized— it's super dope, like a whole thing to go to the board meeting, like the marching band marched to the board meeting which is cool and stuff but then Mr. J put it in a different light for me. He was like, *"They're just pandering."* like first of all the band program got a two weeks/ three weeks notice and no other program did, like no other program was like, *"Your programs gonna be slashed in six months and you can do nothing about it."* So we had this time to generate the support. And Mr. J was explaining to me that they're just pandering, you know? If this group can come and give them a sob story, the board's gonna say, *"Oh we can fix it."* Then if the sports come and give a sob story, which they totally— sports are equally important you know? They're gonna pander and give that. So I think it's just a hard issue because every part of education is so incredibly important that you could find a really sad and fundamental story that's gonna make you want to fund it but. . . yes, to the referendum.

I haven't personally faced any prejudice here, I see it all the time though, for sure. Definitely like microaggressions, like all the time like teachers being incredibly condescending to students of color and not to me and like encouraging me and being super supportive of me and not like to the other end of the spectrum. Just in a general notion, people in general— how they speak to me and how I see them speak over women and people of color is totally, that's like blown my mind this year because I hadn't thought about it much before then. But definitely there will be teachers who speak definitely in a different way. Also: security guards— super weird! Because all the security guards are people of color or most of them are. And every time this year I just walk past them and then there's like a group of kids of color walking the other way and they always go to them. So like that's super weird. And just generally, I think it's super unfortunate that if you want to exhaust your educational resources that means you're gonna be in class with all white people. Like if you want to take advanced courses that means white courses, which is definitely like the— like an education gap between high courses and low courses. Like I remember if you think back freshman/sophomore classes were just different, they were integrated, now they're not, none of my classes are integrated.

I live in a super white neighborhood and all my friends are white, like mostly. So I think living here has made racial disparities a reality and not an option. As opposed to why I totally could go to the French school or North Shore Country Day and I'd get to remove myself from it. But it has made racial disparities a reality and not an option, so I think it's made me understand the necessity for silence for people like me. I'm not too good at it at all— pretty bad at it, but definitely the importance of me speaking less and listening more, I have learned a lot this year. I think also, it's solidified— like I'm a super independent person, I like to think, and it's solidified that, like that idea in my head like super hard because I like come into AM support and like staying after school and like talking to teachers because that's the only way I'll be able to function, I need extra help a lot. So it's bread super independence in me. . . Also like "wokeness" I guess, I don't really like that term, but like, I dunno like social visibility, like being actually able to see things that I wouldn't have been able to see before. Like ETHS has so many extremely smart people in it, that are constantly ready to like attack and check people which is super beautiful I think. And that has definitely shaped my identity. Identity is definitely a term I connotate with people whose identity isn't the constant, you know? Cause I think my identity— I don't have a lot of time to think about my identity, you know, cause it's the constant, the white man's identity. . . I associate that more with people who have to go out of their way to be like, "*What is my identity*?" I don't really have to think about that, which is bad I guess I should. . .

I would like to see realtors going into my neighborhood and showing all different people different places to live in Evanston. Like it really being when you look to live here you get shown every house available, you know? I mean not every house but a house in all the areas. I would like to see our local government more reflective of Evanston, like the people who are progressive, whatever that word means, actually wanting to do stuff because everyone says this stuff about Evanston, but it this semester I've really realized that our politics is pretty similar to U.S. politics. Like with Devon Reid— just the shear resistance of like, "*You can't do this.*" or like, "*I'm gonna do this to you.*" it's just so much, it feels like every week there's just reporter or some s*** coming up to him. I do phone banking and data entry where I take different peoples names and put it into this database and the people who run his campaign are called Reclaim Evanston, or Reclaim Chicago is the bigger one. And those two guys that work there, in the office that I go to, are super cool (and I wanna work there I think) but it's a lot of driving around and stuff, and just really learning that mostly all the city council is white and just I would like to see real change for the people in the city council, calling out like, "*Realtors need to be held accountable, and the police need to be held accountable.*" Okay, that's something: the politics reflecting the community and police accountability in Evanston. Back to the issue of people thinking, "*Oh its post racial.*" like everyone has a high vocabulary about racial issues, like they think it's over, like so many people in Evanston think there's no need for police accountability.

My mom, she's trying to establish— she works for HOW (Housing Opportunities for Women) she's trying to make a low income housing residence in Evanston. And all these people are attacking it— just basically a lot of white people, nowhere near their house at all, feel the need to defend the people who are gonna live there. They're like, "*You're putting them in the s***tiest part of town, and they have no resources there.*" and it's on Dempster and Dodge, like it's a great place to be, like lots of stuff to do. . .

My project has nothing to do with anything I was just talking about. I really wanted to do something activism related but I figured I have college and my whole life to do that, so I might spend these few months doing something I won't be doing as much, which is music. So, I'm making a recording studio in the music wing of ETHS. So there's two rooms, I'm making one the control room, and one a live room, like that are a recording studio and you can like talk in be-tween the two and stuff. So I'm making a recording studio, I'm trying to make a recording club that will meet weekly, so it will meet at the recording studio. The reason that needs to exist is like the only way you can go down there and use that stuff is if you're in a music class. And that entails— like there's no economic barrier because they'll like give you an instrument and give you lessons and everything but it's just like, what if you don't want to read music and play classical music? You know, that's just kinda square, like not everyone's trying to do that. I mean, there's an electronic music class so I'm trying to make it so in the electronic music class there's like a recording por-tion, you know? But I need to have a club because people can't just go down there any time of day and be like, "*Oh I'm with this record-ing club. . .*" because if you see anyone who's not in the program you have to kick them out. Because people steal s*** all the time, and they'll smoke weed in the bathroom and have sex and like de-stroy the whole music wing, it f****** sucks. So yeah, there's a huge security issue, so I'm making a recording club that would meet once a week and do stuff and like record and get other people involved. And I guess I'm trying to measure (because you have to have an es-sential question) "*What's the impact you can have on the program and the community?*" Which I have been doing by giving it a valu-able resource, I guess. Ever since I was a freshman I would look in there and there's like microphones and like a mixing board and a computer and there's actually a window cut between the two rooms, to like look between them cause the person, Dr. Fodor who used to work here and retired six years ago cut that— like had someone cut that a few years before he retired and got a wire connecting the two rooms. So those— those would have taken me months alone and those were already done, so that's where I got the idea from. For the first month I was like cleaning out, moving stuff— I also started before this semester so I started cleaning and moving stuff. There's a lot of administrative stuff, like rules and money and stuff so I meet with the department chair a lot and I meet with the band director a lot. So cleaning, and searching for stuff that I might want to buy, installing these speakers. . . learning how to use the program, learning how to use all the equipment and then training this one kid who's gonna run it next year.

Maya Madjar

So my mom grew up on the southside of Chicago and she was actually part of like a homeless like low income community. And she has had to go through like a lot of stress and trauma, and probably has like PTSD from like living in that community. It's really crazy seeing what a dramatic difference there is in what I had growing up. Like the northside versus the southside, they're like two different worlds. And then she ended up moving to Bloomington which is a smaller town, lower crime rate, cheaper and she likes a lot and I visit her on the weekends. And then my dad, he grew up on the northside of Chicago, which is the same area that I do now. He got to live in like this nice gay, white, higher income, safe neighborhood. And it's just really interesting just comparing the lifestyle differences and the stories and the experiences and how they react to things today. Because like my mom's like more paranoid than my dad, for good reason, because she just grew up in a different community. And my dad lives in Chicago now and I live with him.

So I live with my mom in Normal, Illinois, and that was a Republican small town and there is definitely like regression with the millennials. It was really challenging to grow up in a small town, or be in a small town but also have to be in a Republican small town. And then moving to Evanston— it was like a whole new magical world. I moved here my freshman year and so it was like kind of like— my freshman year was literally just a one year party. And like I was still academically fine but it was just the differences in the people here. . . like I was just so interesting to everyone because I was from a different town and they didn't recognize me. And people were really approachable for me. I know some people don't have that experience, I just got lucky that I got to have that experience of like being extroverted and like being a girl and all of those things. And so freshman year was a blast. My sophomore year was good. One negative experience I can highlight that Evanston will forever have a problem with, unless they actually start moving, is Wellness. My Wellness class— it stressed me out, I had stress dreams about it, I wrote letters to my Wellness teacher telling him about how his curriculum can be triggering or in accurate or a waste of time and he looked at me after he read it and he just said that he has authority and he's been doing his job for years. And I said, "*I'm not the only one that has that opinion.*" And he's like, "*Well you're the only one that's talked to me.*" But like okay. . . that doesn't mean anything, I'm just the only one that's talked to you about it. So that something that I would love to see improvements in. It's incredibly important— sufficient sex-ed and sufficient health and sufficient mental awareness, and no one feels included at all, in Wellness— well I'm sure there's a group of people, but there's definitely questions and discourse and a lot of things that should be talked about with the kids and even if they want to talk about it, they can't because they don't even know about it. Like some sophomores haven't even heard of trans kids, like why isn't that a discussion?

My junior year was good, a huge complaint I had was that I was signed up for AP History even though I didn't want to take it. And so I was taking three AP classes and then I just dropped out of history because I didn't want to be in it, and that's when I realized that like the dynamics behind the counselors, they're just really trying to drive their students. And there should be a certain amount of guidance, because like I don't like making big decisions on my own, but there also should be a certain amount of like, *"Trust yourself. Know yourself, take what feels good."* Because I was taught from like freshman year that I need to go to college and that I need to meet all of this criteria, and that everything is going to follow with me. And now that I'm a senior and applied to college, and got in, like I'm fine. Like I dropped out of my math class, like I have done everything they told me not to and it's fine (and that's not the situation for a lot of people, or some people) but as long as you're doing what makes you happy, you're going to find somewhere that wants you too because that's what you want to do and that's what you're good at. So junior year was a bit atrocious and I felt really pressured, which seems to be a really common topic but it just really upsets me because now that I'm like done it's like, *"Holy s***, none of that was necessary. I don't need any of this, I don't need any of those scare tactics, I don't need to study for hours on end for the ACT because there are schools for everybody."*

And then senior year– senior year's good, I love— the Senior Studies class should forever be a class. There could definitely be improvements, it's just a really large class and that makes it really challenging. There just needs to be more space and more resources. . . because it's growing. Senior Studies has taught me a lot about myself, it's inspired me to take two gap years instead of one, it's built a lot of communities for me, it's made me rethink what my college experience is going to be. Because it could be just classes and work and parties or it could be classes and work and parties and clubs and sports and everything that I like to do. And it doesn't have to be anything I don't want to do. I don't have to join cross country because it's good for college, I can join cross country because I want to do cross-country. So in conclusion, if it wasn't for Senior Studies and if it wasn't for me being lucky and realizing some things about myself before it was too late, I might not be doing two gap years. I might've applied to more rigorous schools even though that's not what I want. And it's just, we really need to change— kids should go to college if they can, but we really need to change the dynamics behind our options and we really need to make it not so black-and-white. And we need to say like— like Ruby, she has a job and she's going to be a chef and she's already been a chef, and she has many items on the menu. And she's not going to college, and that's what she's doing. And I'm not in that place but I'm somewhere in that realm. And so I don't need to go to super rigorous school, I don't need to go for more than four years, like I don't know. . . so. I haven't talked about that college experience with most my friends, it's sort of more like, "*Where are you going to college? Are you happy there? Are you getting scholarships? Awesome.*" There seems to be unanimous agreement that like people need to learn that our school needs to have some different routes and different outlets. As far as pressure being put on kids I'm sure it's on minorities more than ever, I mean for good reason because there's a huge academic gap, there's huge scholarship gaps. . . huge gaps everywhere. But as far as like specific groups, I don't know. I'd say the pressure is half family half school pressure.

Evanston definitely really got me politically involved, it has pushed me far left until I started reevaluating the things that were said to me and I realized that I was there (not my teachers at all, because teachers don't really talk politics) but I was letting my community keep shoving me to the left without me even evaluating the whole situation. And while I would consider myself left I wouldn't consider myself a liberal. . . I wouldn't consider myself a Democrat, I would sort of associate is a socialist. I would call myself left but saying liberal as a term has a lot of. . . it's just too broad for me, it would almost be like identifying with a president— or I don't know, I'm a Bernie Sanders supporter and 90% of the things he says I completely agree with if, not like 100%, but I also like don't know everything yet. Like I don't know the holistic views of everyone and everything. Like I would much rather be called a liberal than like a Republican, because I have just never found myself to agree with most things. But they're still like, worth hearing. . . I also think that liberals can be very blind, I think that liberals have a lot of blind obedience and they really need to focus, because they're focusing on being hyper liberal, and language policing and making sure that their opinion is known, and their opinions are other people's opinions but I think that that's the wrong approach as a stereotypical liberal. But as far as Evanston, they've really given me some positive outlets as to where to start moving in my identity and I would say large part of my identity is political involvement because I spent so much time in political involvement so they've given me an identity in political involvement. But I am just really looking forward to immersing myself in communities that aren't hyper liberal.

In Evanston, first of all, specifically, I would love to see— Mr. Shenk in an interview, I interviewed him and he said, "*Evanston is a lot of talking but not much walking.*" He said it way better than that, I forget exactly what the quote was. But Evanston has a large tendency, which is inevitable in a large school to waste students time in that they make us take classes that we dread. It's just like all of these. . . "idiosyncrasies" I guess is the word, the policies such as like: you have to have your ID, they start closing the doors and you have to get a pass, even though it's all computerized, you can mark students tardy. So it's almost– I'm almost nitpicking but like those things add up in the student's experience because one of the greatest things that defines a good school is a student feeling valuable and that their time is used well and that they are responsible and independent and have purpose. And if we're taking a whole semester class to graduate, and it's a class that we don't want to take then like what are we doing to our students?

So, for my project, I'm doing food waste and redistribution, which is in essence– I'm doing investigative journalism with that. So in essence 40% of our food that we produce is wasted, from farm to grocery store to household. So I'm mainly working in the grocery store sect of that just because I can get large amounts of food and I can make a lot of connections. So, so far, today is March 20th, and I rescued around a ton and a half of food, which would be about 3000 pounds of food. And in that I go to different grocery stores, mainly small grocery stores near my house, I live in Chicago in Lakeview. So I have like Big Apple Finer Foods, and Chipelas (is that how you pronounce it?) there's like a small Mexican grocery store, there's D n' D's on the northside of Evanston. And then I have a couple companies such as Starbucks. . . and gosh– Panera and Dunkin' Donuts, and anyone who caters, if they know me— like I got food from Mayor Daley because he had like leftover food. So, like in essence I just put my name out there and I'm sort of like a grassroots like one person team that just goes around and takes food that's like about to be going to the garbage. And then I read distribute it to the Y and to Streetwise and the Lincoln Park Shelter near my house and sometimes my classmates when I can't find anywhere else to put it. And then I use it for fundraiser dinners to make money, because that's an easy way to bring people together and to get them to pay money. So Ruby and I did a fundraiser dinner, and we got all the food from Big Apple Finer Foods and D n' D's (they did some really large donations for us) and we raised about $800, we hosted 30 people, and so it was a smaller dinner and we're hoping to do a larger dinner soon. We made $800 for DREAMERS club— that's a great thing about our project because it's a really easy way to fundraise. We had potato soup as an appetizer and then tacos and then we had apple cobbler as a dessert, and all the food except for tortillas and butter were from food waste!

And so what I mainly get from grocery stores is a lot of their perishable foods, I get a lot of fruits and veggies which are the highest demand, I know they're the most easily thrown away because if they are slightly blemished they're thrown out automatically. If they are close to expiration date— so for like meats and dairy and eggs, I get a lot of that. And as far as like bigger corporations, they're not cooperating with me because they have corporate above them and they're not really able to tell me anything or don't know anything. But what I've found just like doing a quick search of the back is that they have really large compactors, and the compactors in an essence— they fill food with it and I've seen this in documentaries- they fill food with it (and a lot of it comes from overstock) because when you go to a grocery store they never run out of anything be-cause they're buying too much food, and will take the fresh food and they just smash it down and I mean, just make it into like mush, and then you can see like the mush, like spilling out a little bit, and you can see like all the fresh food— like all the different colors and there will be like tomatoes and apples and plums, like spilling over, that like didn't get in. And like I don't even want to know what's going in there. But what I do know is that the donation they do that– I've gotten like boxes and boxes of mac & cheese and cereals if they're like slightly damaged, then they're not selling and they get thrown out. There's a lot bigger issue of just laziness as to why this isn't getting re-distributed because there's just laws. . . And I don't even know I haven't done a ton of research yet, but I just been trying to bring awareness to the food waste epidemic and do what I can do my part while I'm here for the time being.

Shirine Marzouki

My parents were born in Tunisia, so that's a country in North Africa. And they came here– my dad came here specifically because he had a son (from a different marriage) and he wanted to be close to him. And my older brother lived in Sheboygan at that time. So, it's really hard because my dad was like, *"I'm not living in Sheboygan, h*** nah!"* So, he needed a place where we could continue our French and be within a Tunisian community and be close to my brother, so there was like a lot of like. . . prerequisites. And so he just like landed on Evanston because he heard about it through like, people talking. And he was looking at different apartments and they gave him the ones on the southside so that's just like where we landed, and I'm so happy we did so. . . yeah.

I think like when I think of ETHS being authentic and maybe. . . real was like during the Calvin Terrell assembly just because like everyone was shaken by it like no matter how privileged you are or unprivileged you are. That's like the time where everyone was questioning who their identity was and for him to be like, "*Yeah you guys have been told all of this and you have to deal with it every day.*" It was a pretty amazing experience to feel like an outsider but like everyone was feeling like an outsider so like it was pretty dope. Know what I mean? It felt really like, raw for everyone to feel the same way.

So my first day— I went to Chute first of all, I'm such a southside girl, and it was really weird because my house is on the border of Nichols and Chute so it was very strange to come home and people were like, "*Boo you Chute. . .*" So there was this new kind of. . . attachment to a school that I had never felt before. So like being "Chute Pride" meant something, and that was something I had to work on myself, like what does "Chute Pride" mean to me? I have been really lucky to have landed in Chute, because being white was the minority. So me being a person of color, it was just great because I was able to be– not be in a white space for the first time in my life. And I just got to know so many people. . . from so many different backgrounds, through like great classes like drama class, you know, and like where we interpreted "Raisin in the Sun" and that's how I met Lauren Davis. And she's such an inspiration to me to this day, so yeah.

Of course I've seen prejudice. Anywhere you live, I feel like you'll encounter it. How have I handled it— like for me sometimes it's just going home and crying. . . and writing about it in my journal. And sometimes when I would see it, it would be me standing up and sometimes it would just be watching it. Nowadays (like this year and recently) it was mostly like— there was a fight that happened a couple months ago and I started to scream at my math class because it was right outside of our classroom and I was like, "*If you guys are gonna show up for the fight are you going to show up for the funeral as well*? Like, "*Why is this entertaining you*?" Like, "*These two indi-*

viduals are physically harming each other and you're just laughing about it." So, that felt very disappointing in my community, because I was like, "We are better than this we shouldn't be just watching people hurt themselves." And actually Hugo. . . he was physically like trying to like rip the two apart and to me that was so heroic. And I was on the other side like screaming at others, so like that was fantastic, like for me as a leader but I was also just like very disappointed in my people because, I call Evanston– like everyone's my brother and sister.

I'd like Evanston to kind of own up to our flaws. Just because like a lot of times, as Amanda would say, "We are fake as h***." Like we are so ridiculously kind of stuck and like love the status quo. And sometimes it feels good to just be like, "Yeah we're messed up, and that's OK, let's work on that." You know? And like owning up to our. . . just redlining, in general would be one step forward to actually creating change in the community because time and time again we have stopped: creating a school in the Fifth Ward or we have stopped development on the south side of Evanston, you know what I mean? There are so many things that have not created change because we haven't even owned up– we just prefer to just ignore the problem, instead of actually dealing with it and not just spending money on it, you know what I mean? And I think like Chute is a great example of that just because like our principal understands and like any discipline issue we have at that school is dealt with by him, so he understands firsthand how to, you know, challenge his students and react and inter-react with his students. So by the end of the year, you were like, it feels like a family, and not just like peers that you're gonna see in the next ten years. I'm mean like Hazel, I met her my first year there and I'm still friends with her, you know what I mean? And it's funny because like, when you watch those middle school movies you think, "Oh I'm not gonna be friends with them. . ." but funny enough most of my friends from high school are from Chute so it's pretty amazing to like own up to what is missing and then like work from there. Which like we still have some problems with.

My project is leadership through the perspective of a woman and so I just held the Women's Empowerment Conference two weeks ago, where we rallied 120 students who identified as female to Northwestern. And kind of deconstructed sexism, feminism and kind of all of the conditioning we as women have had to deal with every day. It was really amazing and again this is where we had to encounter a different kind of prejudice because we had to make it clear that, "*Yes we are women we all, you know, face a certain oppression, but many of us have a different battle to fight, and are more oppressed than others.*" And so really drilling intersectionality, and so when we talked about prejudice there was this girl who said, "*Why are we talking about race so much at a gender conference?*" So, we had to like reiterate why, you know so yeah…*laughs*. It was complicated, and thank god Ms. Mac was there, and many of the women of color like went into a bathroom and we all had a conversation within each other. And to many that felt empowering, but also I felt like I betrayed my sisters, because I promised and I worked my a** off to create an intersectional conference. Like I made sure that I did not want whiteness present, but somehow whiteness crashed my party. So it was just handling that afterwards, we had to deconstruct why we're talking about race so much, because you can't have a conversation about social justice without incorporating race. So I think it went well, it inspired a bunch of people to go to S.O.A.R next year (which is great) and think more about their white privilege.

Stuart McKean

My mom was born in Milwaukee, Wisconsin, uh, in 1963 and my dad was born in Providence, Rhode Island, he grew up in Louisville, Kentucky for his entire life. So after college— they both went to the University of North Carolina, and being from the South and living very close to— well Chicago is essentially the biggest city in any proximity to Louisville, and my dad just kind of wanted to work there. And Chicago is always sort of a destination if you're from Milwaukee so they ended up here. I dunno they met when they were in their 20's and they sort of lived throughout the different neighborhoods in the city and they had me and my brother, and I dunno, here we are today.

I think one of the really cool things about going to school here is that I get to meet a lot of people— not necessarily through. . . how do I put this. . . like class not necessarily, but like what I mean by that is that I don't meet them through the curriculum of the class but like based off of their opinion and like what they bring to, each sort of thing that happens in high school. Some negative things about ETHS would be. . . I feel that where we go to high school ignores a lot really important aspects of having open conversations about many problems that we face in Evanston and in the whole country.

I've lived here since seventh grade, so I think that my experience has been a bit more. . . for lack of a better word. . . "sheltered" than a lot of other peoples. Like I don't know, it's really interesting to go through Senior Studies and like, we were talking about "six degrees of separation" and like people that other people know, I just don't have the connections that a lot of people in Evanston have, so that's kinda really interesting. I just don't feel as ingrained in the community as other people— simply because I didn't grow up here, it's not that I don't feel a part of the community, I'm just not from here. I would say that people who have grown up here, like this is— like it's theirs, like you can tell who's "Old Evanston" versus someone who hasn't lived here their entire lives.

I would just like to see Evanston more, sort of— actually this is actually kind of interesting: I was having a really cool conversation last night about comparing Germany and America. And what makes Germany thrive so much now, is that they're incredibly ashamed of their past and what makes America so s***** is that it's not. So I think that if Evanston could just open up about the non-sugar coated history that it has, then I feel like we'd have a much easier time fixing and then celebrating our community in the future.

So my project is. . . I'm making a short film that has to do with— sort of teenage substance abuse in our community. Well my original project idea was— well I knew I wanted to make a movie, and I had just seen this movie called "Manhattan" Woody Allen made in the 70's and its sort of like this really stunning, like visually poetic love letter to Manhattan. So I was thinking like, *"Oh I kind of want to do like an Evanston story through this visually poetic lens."* So I was like, *"Oh I need to get a better feel for Evanston, simply because I haven't lived here as long."* And then I interviewed a ton of people and what I found, interviewing particularly people who are my age, like my peers, is that getting caught up in substance abuse is actually a huge problem here. It's something that I think is a story that needs to be told and I could still have that sort of visual element of having Evanston as like the backdrop for it. I wouldn't say it's necessarily like an anti-drug thing, it's more of an anti-substance abuse thing. And that— that's my project. Most of the people that I interviewed were women, so. . . the lead is a woman. I tried to make it diverse, to sort of speak to the diversity within Evanston. So there's two women and there's a black man and then a non-binary person as well. I held some auditions and then I had some people who were curious about it come up to me and they were like, *"I'm totally interested in reading for this!"* and I was like, *"Okay awesome!"*

Emma Milner-Gorvine

So my dad was born in Philadelphia, Pennsylvania, and my mom was born in Nebraska or Nevada (I can never keep those two straight) but was born there because they were like living there for like a year but then she moved back— she moved to Milwaukee when she was like three months old (so she's from Milwaukee). My entire family on her side lives in Milwaukee, or like, California. Those are the two places. Or Israel. One of the three! But yeah, they both went to Earlham College which is in Richmond, Indiana, which is where they met. They started dating their second semester freshman year which is really terrifying to me *laughs* and so they were in, like my mom always was in the Midwest and my dad went to school in the Midwest.

Then they moved to Philly for a little bit and were by my dad's parents and then they moved— my dad did grad school at University of Michigan and they moved to Ann Arbor and then I was born in Ann Arbor and my dad was looking for work. He had a PhD and he wanted to teach. He likes— he teaches psychology at Northwestern and he likes psychology but he loves teaching, he could have gone into any subject I think, and been happy as long as he was teaching. And he got a job at Aurora, or maybe first Argosy, in Chicago and my mom had a criteria for where they were going to move, specifically having to do with the Jewish community. There had to be a reform synagogue that had a full-time rabbi, full-time youth director and full-time cantor. So, Evanston met the criteria with Beth Emet. That's where we go now. We went to Beth Emet a little bit and then we switched to Sukkat Shalom which is up in Wilmette or something and then we switched back. It was a long story— unnecessary story. But, so, Evanston met the criteria and people know about Evanston it's well known, it's diverse, all those things and my parents really wanted me to grow up somewhere like that so they bought an apartment in Evanston and that's how we ended up here, when I was three.

Well I love ETHS. I have plenty of issues with ETHS, but I think I've really enjoyed high school overall. Even now, even second semester senior year. I guess one of the really weird things about coming to high school— I went to Oakton, and then Chute, which are the two most heavily low-income schools in Evanston. Like Oakton is the most for elementary schools and Chute is the most for middle schools which translates fairly directly to most "not white" unfortunately. So, it was really weird coming to ETHS because my first reaction was, "Where did all these white girls come from?" Like, "What is going on?" And it was weird because, I'm a white girl but it wasn't— you know Chute is 60% not white and Oakton is 75%, so it was very different. Like I felt like I was walking into New Trier it was really weird for me. Especially like, as high school progressed and you specialize more and more and like I took AP classes which are fairly segregated so that was one of my first memories of ETHS is coming here and being like, "Why are there so many white people?" and like, "*Where did they all come from?*" I guess North Evanston *laughs*.

I guess positive experiences have been, it's just such a big school that you can really find your passion. I took a wide-range of classes. I took engineering freshman year and I took ceramics sophomore year and I did ChemPhys and then I was like, "*I don't like this.*" I stopped after sophomore year it was too much— so I've had a lot of opportunities here. I finished Spanish last year so classes-wise it was a really positive experience. For the most part people here are friendly. I think as you get older, like sophomore/junior year people get less friendly. And then senior year everyone feels guilty, they're all like, "*Say hi to someone new!*", "*Say hi to a senior you haven't met before!*" and it's like, "*Where did all this come from?*"

I remember freshman year (so I'm like 5 feet tall. . . *laughs* about the same height I still am now) and I was walking through the hallway and this one kid said to the other kid, "*Aw dude, that's so gay.*" And I was like, I'm going to evaluate this situation and see if I should interject and I decided like, that it was a good situation to interject. And this kid is like a 6 foot 2 black guy and I'm just like, "*Do you mean happy?*" like "*I'm happy! Gay means happy!*", and he goes "*What the f*** short white girl.*" *laughing* and I was like, "*I don't know, big black guy.*" and then he laughed and walked away. So I like to think that he doesn't use gay as an insult anymore but it was a really funny experience. That was one of my favorite things, like honestly one of the best moments in high school, so I guess I peaked freshman year. I'm trying to think of other positive experiences— Senior Studies I guess. Senior Studies has been the most recent positive experience, just getting to study what you want to study and really getting to dive in and meet new people. I guess negative experience wise— I really don't like how segregated ETHS is, and I don't know how to fix it, I don't think one person can. I don't like how segregated the classes are, especially AP's like there's not any way to get around it, um, yeah that's always been a big thing at ETHS.

So like I said I went to Oakton and then Chute. I loved elementary school, I did the TWI program (the Two Way Immersion Spanish Program). In kindergarten, I came home crying for like a solid two months because I didn't understand what was going on in school, cause they were like (they've loosened it a lot, I think recently) but it was like 90% Spanish when I started, like it was like you learned how to read and write in your native language, so the native Spanish speakers learned how to read and write in English and we learned how to read and write in Spanish. But like they only talked to us in Spanish, and I remember like my teacher, who was like this white woman from Ann Arbor had me like 100% convinced she didn't speak English, like for all of the first few months. And I remember I tripped and fell on some pavement, at recess, and you know, I had like scabs on my knees and my elbows and she comes up and she's like, "*Emma are you okay?*" and I was like, "*You speak English??*" So I think TWI is a really different experience than any other program. Oakton also— I think when I was in 2nd or 3rd grade developed the ACC which is Afro Centric Curriculum, so I think Oakton is a really different environment than most places. I remember we would go to Afrocentric assemblies and they would teach us different African words, there was always a Kwanzaa festival. I recently went back to Oakton for Senior Studies (because we couldn't visit New Trier last minute) and there was a lot of stuff about strong African American figures in history and implementing the stuff that you wouldn't learn. Otherwise, it has created a lot of issues in Oakton— in my opinion. It's pretty much all black students, which— it is what it is, but I think it's a little bit problematic, and there are more non-white students than white students so it makes sense, but I think it just segregates a little more. Which is already what kids tend to do themselves, by the end of elementary school. But there are a lot of interesting aspects to it. I think it created a lot of tension between TWI and ACC, because there was always this feeling of, "*Oh there's not enough resources for both of us. Which one of us is gonna go?*" Which I don't think was true, but that's the type of tension it created— mostly among teachers but also amongst students.

But yeah, TWI was a lot of cultural immersion. I thought that I was Latina for a while, like I was like, "*Yup, I'm Mexican.*" and my parents were like, "*No, no you're not.*" and I was like, "*. . .are you sure?*" Cuz it was just a lot of like— we went to Pilsen several times a year, and we celebrated Three Kings Day (I think that's what it's called, I can't even remember any more) but it was just a lot of cultural immersion. And it also was. . . it was hard. We had a lot of kids get deported mid-year— we had one kid get deported mid-year, that I can still really remember. It was 5th grade, and he came from Guatemala, and he came for a month and a half maybe and then he was gone, and his whole family was gone. So I guess I can't totally assume that's what it was but he wasn't like, "*Oh, bye guys I'm going to Chicago.*" He just wasn't there. It was just really weird— it was very unreal.

I think in 4th and 5th grade was when there became a divide between the white and the Latino kids. Because we didn't have any African American kids, you were either white, or you were Mexican, we had a couple kids from Ecuador but that was kinda it. And so that was kinda the divide and I think the divide really became apparent in like 4th and 5th grade, and that's kind of when people started to leave and not come back. Which was something that a lot of the non-white kids in my class had already experienced, and we hadn't. Like as much as I was like, "*I'm Latina!*" when I was little, I wasn't.

I really loved TWI though, my sister's in TWI now (she's six years younger than me) and there's way less Spanish which makes me really sad. Well I guess she's in sixth grade now, so she's not in TWI anymore. But the high school experience with Spanish has been interesting (because they created a TWI class right after I started high school) so I took Spanish 3 Honors as a freshman and then finished 5 AP last year. So I was just pushed ahead instead of actually put in a TWI class and I wasn't put in the heritage class (because I'm not a native Spanish speaker). I think there's a lot less Spanish now because of testing, and you know, they have to do well on tests. And when I was in 3rd grade the native Spanish speakers took their tests in Spanish until the teacher decided— like if they decided in 4th grade or 5th grade like, "*Oh you can do this in English.*" like, "*You can take the ISAT in English.*" But now they all have to take it in English, so there's a lot more of a push to get the English in, which there wasn't when I was there. And I think with the testing— I don't want to see programs like TWI or even ACC, I think ACC is flawed, I think TWI is also flawed, but I don't want to see them go away. And I think especially with the language immersion of TWI, the Spanish is going away. And I think that's a big asset that we'd lose.

And then at Chute— I loved Chute. I really like school, I'm that kid, so I really liked Chute. I think the principal does a really good job of like containing all of that middle school bullying and drama that everyone usually has. I think Chute was where there was like the white girls table and the white boys table and the black boys table and the black girls table and the Latino boys table and the Latina girls table, and I think that's when there was a like really big divide. Because like up until 5th grade, you know, we were all in the same class, all day every day, you had to be friends with people. But in 6th grade you are in a whole bunch of different classes, and there are new people from other schools, and only two out of the three schools that feed into Chute have TWI. We did have Spanish together— there was TWI Spanish, so that kept the group kind of together but it fell apart by high school. Like I say, "Hi." to people in the hallways and that's kind of it.

As a white person I haven't experienced racism. But being Jewish, I would say yes, I have faced some prejudice in Evanston, but it's really different. Cause it's not as blatant, it's not as in your face, like I've never had someone be like, "AHH kill all of the Jews." other than in jokes, which still isn't okay but, you know it's a little bit of a different thing. I started to notice it a lot more in high school, like especially the "special" brand of left wing anti-Semitism that stems a lot from Israel and Israel's behavior, which is a whole other topic. But there's a lot of, you know, associating Jews with Israel, like all Jews with Israel. Or if you even think Israel should even exist, but you're still slightly critical of the whole government. . . you can't say that. So I started to notice that a lot more junior and senior year, I became much more educated on Israel, I went to Israel the past summer. And also I was talking with my mom recently, and I didn't realize this but I do remember kids telling me like, "Oh you're gonna go to Hell." And when I was little I was like, "Oh they just don't understand, they're just religiously different, they'll get older and they won't say things like that." Like I remember being a little upset about it, but when it's a regular thing that is said to you, you have to not be upset about it. And my mom was like, *"You don't think that was anti-Semitism?"* And I hadn't really thought about it until my mom was like, *"It kind of is."* So there's been stuff like that or *"You're the first Jew I've ever met."* (which is very rare in Evanston) but you still get it all the time. So yeah, I guess there's some underlying anti-Semitism that Evanston doesn't really address. But there's definitely a big Jewish community that has helped me in. . . not being angry. I think that Jewish history is a little bit of history that aligns more with African American history, even though a lot of Jews are white. So it's really interesting that it's not racial, but it is. . . you know, like Holocaust was definitely racial, and like where do we stand now? Cause it doesn't just go away— like we know that with racism, it doesn't just go away because we have integrated schools. . . now there's no more slavery, it doesn't just go away. So where's the anti-Semitism in Evanston? It's still here it's just not as easy to find, I think.

Okay so for my project, I am writing a book on youth activism and reproductive rights. So far it's been a lot of service and a lot of research— I have an internship, the Tendam for Mayor campaign, which ends in two weeks. The election is in two weeks, so once people vote that's it. There, I've been doing a lot of administrative work, a lot of phone banking. . . which is unpleasant, but has to get done. One day I spent the entire three hours— I thought it was going to take one hour— it took three, taking precincts from the last contested mayoral race (which was a long time ago because we've had Tisdahl for a long time) and then trying to see where these precincts line up with the precincts now, because they have changed. But there was no clear map of how they were changed. So I had to take them, and map it out and kind of figure out where you get the most voter outcome. And so it took me like three hours, and it was really interesting because most of— the most voter outcome was north Evanston. And I was not surprised, I was disappointed. So that was really interesting. And then I've been doing service at the Democratic Office where I've been doing phone banking and stuff to oppose the Trump Administration.

Elinor **Montgomery**

So my project is a research based project, with community service that's like. . . completely unrelated. So I do community service at Park, and I go two to three times a week, and it's like totally unrelated but I love it so much, and like I couldn't stop going. We do a lesson plan so like usually we will just do like the lesson of the day, and I work in a classroom from kids who are like— it's for like severely cognitively disabled kids, so it's like 11 to 13, but they have very low conative capability and most of them have physical disabilities too. So we do lessons about vocabulary, so it will be like a geography lesson about vocabulary and it will be like, "*travel. . . globe. . . earth. . .*" like really basic words like that. And for a lot of them it's getting them to look at something or like touch something if they're physically able, and a lot less of like, "*Can they comprehend it?*" But it's really cool, and like I had no experience working with disabled kids of any kind, like cognitively or physically before, so I really like that and that's made me more comfortable with that. . . Sorry that was completely unrelated— my project is about like "Fourth Wave Feminism" and "Neoliberalism" kind of, with respect to like older generations. . . and adults and kind of. . . the semantic drift. . . and it's kind of all over the place honestly. But right now I'm organizing a conversation with adults and teachers in the building about current gender politics, just to like brush up, because I've noticed that a lot of those views by those people: teachers, my parents and grandparents, like the older people I know, are kind of outdated. I'm talking about trans rights mostly and how "Trans Exclusionary Feminism" plays a really big role in "White Feminism", and how "White Feminism" isn't Feminism. So yeah, it's mostly about trans politics and stuff and less about gender roles, you know?

I don't think I really understood fully what this class was about before I took it, and I think I just took it because of the second semester project. But I really— like almost my favorite part of it was like the first semester, and just like learning so much that I didn't know already about Evanston history. And like we like to think of Evanston as like a really inclusive, racially diverse place, but it's not really the case and like our diversity is kind of not genuine, you know? And kind of forced. . . But, yeah, that was probably my favorite part: the first semester.

I mean I wouldn't want to go anywhere else for high school, and I can't really imagine going anywhere else because I've never been anywhere else. . . And I think that ETHS tries really hard to be like as inclusive to everybody as we can, but with that comes a lot of like. . . hype about liberalism, especially in Evanston and a lot, a lot, a lot of neoliberalism and kind of conservative values. So a lot of the views by like rich Evanstonians are fiscal conservatism, which is like— it does not benefit people of color or lower income people, which doesn't benefit a wide population of Evanstonians, obviously.

And so, I dunno, I feel like Evanston liberalism is kind of contrived and in-genuine in a lot of cases. But yeah, I think ETHS tries to be as inclusive as possible which is really nice, and obviously we're getting more and more inclusive as time goes on.

I think Evanston has made me, definitely more liberal and creative. My family moved here from Rogers Park when I was in kindergarten, and if they financially could have, they would have sent me to Waldorf. My parents are really artistic, very like, kinda weird, kookie Evanstonians. And I think that has shaped my identity as much as being in Evanston has. . . and having the outlet for creativity and stuff. And it's a lot more accepted here than I feel like other places, to be different, though there is a limit to that, like there's a limit to how different you can be, before it gets "weird", you know, socially? Which I definitely struggled with early in elementary school and stuff, because my family is like— my mom is an artist, and. . . I dunno we just have a kind of strange-ish family. . . compared to others, I feel like. For fun I like sewed and stuff, and made my own stuffed animals and stuff like that. Which, at the time, felt kind of "uncool" in my elementary school, and I really wanted like a Northface and Uggs and stuff. And now in high school, it feels like suppressing all of that didn't do me like the greatest— like it did me an injustice. . . because now I feel like it's a lot more accepted to be different, in high school.

I definitely want to change the property taxes, because they make it really hard for people to live in Evanston, especially in different places, it really segregates Evanston. And also white people just don't really care for people of color, and because they don't live near them or they don't really experience people of color, I feel like we just don't care as much, as we should. And if affects the politics, it affects like Evanston politics and. . . I dunno. It's also interesting considering the referendum*, right now, because it would increase taxes a lot, which white people are okay with because they can afford it. So like white Evanstonians are like totally for the referendum, which I completely understand, if it didn't pass it would cut, like, the band program I was in for like five years. I dunno, I think it's really interesting and I'm sure a lot of well off white families will vote for it but maybe people of color and the fifth ward won't because like their school didn't have the resources anyway.

*The 2016 referendum was for an increased property tax to fund the District 65 schools

Jameson Ogunbola

My project is basically. . . two folds— it's in two parts. So, the first part of my project is just like— would sort of just be like a traditional PowerPoint, um, talking about the misconceptions of Africa. Every-one knows I'm extremely proud to be Nigerian and African, and I feel like there's so many people that don't understand what Africa is truly about, and how beautiful it is. And like, the only source of in-formation they get about Africa is from the media. And the media's so skewed when it comes to talking about Africa. I feel like if you were to ask a random person like, *"What do you think of Africa?"*, they'd probably say like, *"Starving kids. . . or AIDS. . ."* or *"terrorist attacks. . ."* and Africa's so much more than that. And so I'm gonna be talking about five to seven misconceptions about Africa, that's the first part. And then the second part: I've interviewed various Africans: adults, children of Africans, students and I just asked them questions on why they so proud to be African. How has— how has being African shaped them to be who they are today? And trying to refute the negative connotations that the media like perpetuates about Africans and Africa. And then having actual Africans say like, their own viewpoint from their own experience. . . and you can see like it's very— you can see the two— like the answers and what the media shows are vastly different, and they show two different sides of Africa.

I think Evanston is a decent place. I feel like sometimes, I dunno, people are just so complacent with like "*Evanston is diverse. . .*" and all that, that people don't really fully see that yeah it is diverse, but there are still a lot of different nuances and like different problems in Evanston, especially in Evanston Township High School. Like, we all go to one big school, I guess, but it's so clique-y. I mean it's like we're all like one big melting pot, but the person that you're feeding is like separating the food— if that makes sense. It's like one big melting pot but like people just pick and choose who they wanna be with. And I don't feel like everyone's like really comfortable with each other even though we preach it, even though we post it on Facebook. People are just— people are just like comfortable with the people that they're comfortable with— and that's normally from the same race.

I dunno, this is kinda funny to me but like, I used to think that back in Haven that like. . . all the attractive, like "nice girls" or whatever didn't really like black boys. I dunno why. And, um, like you'd see all of the nice girls, or whatever (we all know who they are) I guess coming from Haven, like they only liked a certain type of boy. And it made me feel insecure, because maybe like— it's like maybe they don't find other people who don't look like that, like seem like that type of boy— as like attractive. Or— I was just insecure about myself. And now it's like at the high school, I've grown up and everyone else has grown up, and I feel like people are more accepting. . . of like finding others attractive— like are more aware of other attractive people besides white people. Basically that's just like one experience I've had.

I think Evanston made me, not necessarily who I am today, but it helped me become more confident in myself. I mean, Evanston's mostly white, and I've gone to mostly white schools my whole entire life. Especially in elementary school— I went to Lincolnwood— really white. And I've always been like, some of the only couple of black kids in like honors classes or AP courses or whatever. And it's really just like strengthened my skin and my character to know? That I know my value and I know my worth, and even though I don't look like most people that are in my classes or that I walk the street with, I'm thinking the same thing to myself.

Alyssa Olagbegi

My dad was born in Nigeria and my mom was born somewhere in Indiana, northwest. . . like Gary or somewhere, I honestly have no clue. But yeah we moved to Atlanta when I was six— from here. And then we came back when I was a sophomore.

One thing that I noticed here was that everybody had a lot of f****** dogs and I don't know why. Everywhere I looked somebody was walking their dog and I thought it was so weird, I mean I lived in a neighborhood in Atlanta where everybody had a dog you— you just didn't walk them because everyone had big a** yards. The diversity here didn't really affect me because I used to live in an all black neighborhood but I was used to diversity because my family is diverse— so it wasn't like a culture shock. Another thing that I noticed is that everybody wore Birkenstocks, at least all the white girls wore Birkenstocks— I thought that was really weird. . . but I have a pair now so I can't like say anything. . .

I don't know it seems like everybody fell into a category, which sounds weird, but like looking on the outside they were so clear. This is so weird, but like, the categories were. . . like I don't want to say the north Evanston kids, but like the super entitled Evanston people. . . which are mostly rich white kids (not all rich white kids but most of them are). And then the kids that kind of fall in the middle, in like the middle of Evanston. . . they're not like super wealthy but they're well off and they're more like. . . "woke". . ? Some of them are still like ignorant. And then towards the bottom of Evanston there are kids who are like, I don't want to say, "trying to be black" or "be ghetto" because then I'll sound like an a**hole. . . I dunno in my head it makes more sense. This literally like goes all along Evanston, like if I could have a map of Evanston right now. . . Like here *motions to North Evanston* are the white kids, like literally, and then like here *motions to South Evanston* are the Howard Street kids. . . like the kids who grow up on that side who are mainly Black and Hispanic and minorities. And like there are exceptions, but like that's just how it plays out. And I don't know I just feel like everybody falls into one of these boxes. . . it's so weird to explain. . . I just remember thinking like, "*I can't tell you guys apart. . . you all act the same.*" And maybe it's because you've lived in Evanston and the Evanston bubble is a real thing but like you all act the same.

The Evanston's bubble is fragile as f***. Like I was saying earlier, Evanston is fake inclusive. . . and I think it's because of that bubble— well most people expect you to act liberal, and to act a certain way and have certain views. . . and if you don't have those views it's like, "*Oh, okay we're going to give you s*** for it.*" because you're breaking the bubble. Like, I don't know, I just want to talk to people who don't have those views and ask them why they think and feel like that. . . but I feel like they'd think I'm attacking them. And I feel like in this town there's this expectation of like, "*Yeah you can do what you* *want. You can do what you want. But just like. . . fall in your box that was already made for you before you even had a choice to say so!"*

Living in Evanston has taught me my life motto which is literally *do whatever the f*** you want.* Like I say this all the time and people don't get it, but please if you're listening to this just live your life G, don't let anybody tell you, you can't do anything. Like living here there's so many different people out there living their lives, doing whatever they want to do, and they're living for themselves and it's the most amazing thing— when you decide that you can just be you and be open. Like me, I just do whatever the f*** I want. I don't care, I'm not going to go out and act like dangerous. . . but I'm not going to hide who I am. . . just so another person isn't like offended or feels some type of way. Like living in Evanston has just taught me to be myself because people are going to like you for who you are. . . and if they don't then that's their loss. And I feel like you can't really be someone who's independent or different if you're not yourself. . . which sounds like super basic, but like yeah.

I feel like in Evanston I've learned just to be like more open-minded. . . like I don't know I catch myself now when I say ignorant s***, or like do something that's like stupid. Even though I say like, *"Don't give a f*** and do what you gotta do."* still, like don't be an a**hole. Be nice, like be caring. . . know who you are but also recognize that you're sharing this world with other people.

The ETHS administration is ridiculous they make exceptions for certain people with like contracts. . . and what gets handled and what doesn't. . . who gets disciplined and what type of discipline they get. . . I don't want to say it's sexist or racist but that's what it seems like. It's giving the wrong people the better outcome. Like the whole thing that happened with Jaylyn and Annie. . . like they were literally walking and they got harassed as freshman, and like that's terrifying. And like nothing happened, the administration did nothing. I don't know, it's just really weird— the way things get handled. And especially in the community that so "inclusive". . . I don't know. . . there needs to be better responses. because we're supposed to be prepared to deal with these things. . . so why can't we just attack these issues that happen? When we clearly have the resources to do it. Like why aren't we utilizing them?

I don't know if people are going to agree with this but like there should be a bigger police presence just because I feel like EPD doesn't do its job. And when they do it's in the wrong places. There are times when I've gone from like deep in Skokie to my house which is by the lake in 10 minutes. . . by speeding. . . and like s*** like that, like it just makes me feel like *"Y'all aren't looking out for me! Like pull me over something let me know you're here!"* I don't know, I just know for a fact that I see more of a police presence on Howard than I do on Central.

My project is— I'm making an EP, which is focusing on the empowerment of black women. So I'm making 3 songs, and they're basically in the style of Nicki Minaj-ish. It's really targeting the whole hip hop genre but also black men because there's a really big divide between black women and men. Basically how black men treat black women, so it's kind of like *"Yo, you can have a preference but remember you need to respect us the way you respect your black mother that birthed you."* Also coming for rappers who call us like "b****es" and "h**s" and stuff like that. . . so it's pretty dope. I produce all the beats myself and I use Logic Pro and GarageBand, and yeah I'm gonna produce and master it.

Amanda Peña

My mom was born in Guatemala City, Guatemala and my father was born in Chicago. My parents and I moved to Evanston because my parents' house is being foreclosed. . . because my aunt just— whatever, payments and whatever. So I ended up in Evanston.

Well, being at Evanston Township has been like a really different experience for me. I was never like, pushed to go to college when I was younger, going to like a CPS school it's not something that they. . . kind of, help you envision for your future. So you know being in Evanston Township is really helped me a lot. I was at Scammon Elementary, but first I was at Trumbull Elementary from pre-k to 6th grade, and then 6th grade through 8th I was at Scammon but I graduated from Chute. Trumbull is not too far from here, it's in Edgewater so, you know. And then Scammon was around my old neighborhood, so there were definitely disparities around the resources that each of the schools had. And then when I got to Chute it was like. . . the biggest disparity that I saw.

So I don't like Evanston— I don't like Evanston a lot, for many reasons. For one, I'm used to being around people of my ethnicity, and so when I moved to Evanston there where— I mean I live in South Evanston which is predominantly Hispanic and African American so I guess that helped but, when I would look at different communities (which is like what I'm doing my project on) I saw a whole bunch of basically, you know, housing discrimination among the different communities that were separated based off of race. It just— it bothers me so much.

I've definitely seen prejudice here. I work at the Jewel on Howard and McCormick, I'm a cashier (my boss is looking to promote me pretty soon) but some days I'll be walking around the isles, you know, putting stuff back or I'll be bagging for someone else. And it gets pretty busy. And I'll notice that people who are not of color, will come to the cashier— well I only bag for one cashier. . . she's my favorite whatever, but she is white and so if I say "Hi." before she does, they automatically turn and say "Hi." to her first. And it's just so weird. And yeah I mean there have been several instances where I was asked if I spoke English and. . . it was crazy.

Living here has definitely made me more proud to be Hispanic. Not only to just be Hispanic but to be Guatemalan. Again living in an area where I see people who are similar to me everywhere, I kind of didn't know how special my identity was until I got here.

I would like Evanston to stop priding themselves on their diversity. Because, you know, there's definitely difference between being diverse and like integrating yourselves and whatever. But definitely that needs to change a lot.

So my project is— I will be doing a 30-minute expose on redlining in Evanston. So in the research that I've been doing I've found that in like among different middle schools there's like— there are clear areas around each that are predominately some kind of race but what I also have found is that you can't disconnect the income disparity with the housing discrimination disparity: it's like the same thing. And I will be visiting a real estate office with a with a black person and a white person (not at the same time, like at different times). With the same budget in mind and then we're basically going to see where they take each of us.

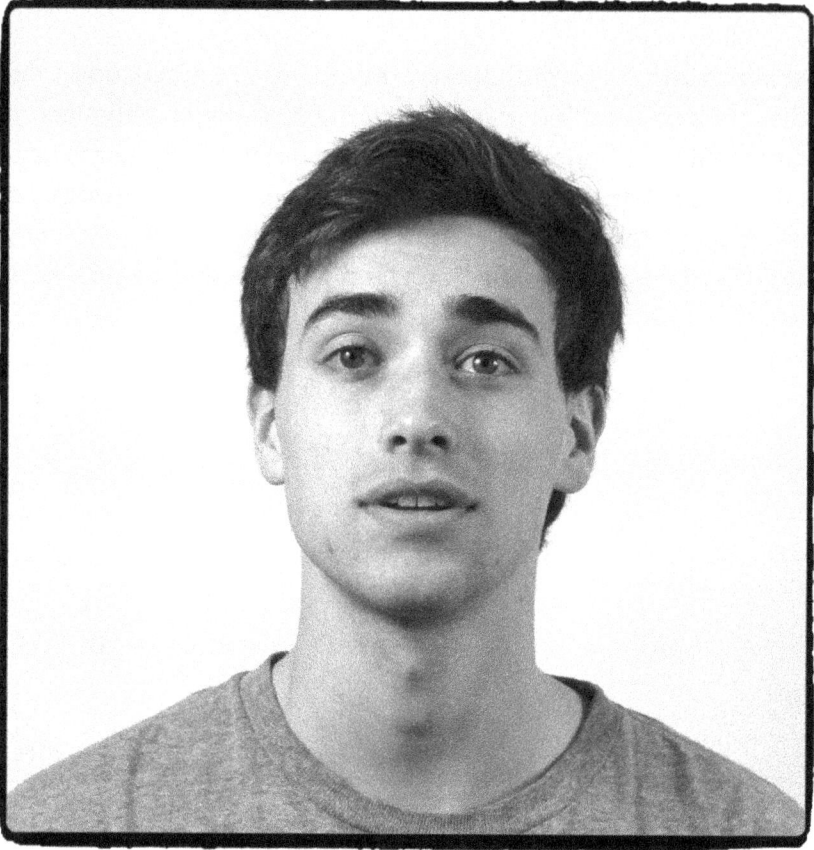

Alex Rohner

My mom was born in Wilmette, and she went to New Trier. . . and my dad was born in Skokie, I think. My dad moved around to a lot of different places, my grandparents are like Swiss immigrants and they always had to move for my grandpa's work. But I'm pretty sure he was born in Skokie and he lived in Skokie for a while and eventually in Winnetka for a while. My parents met at New Trier, and I'm honestly not sure why they came back to Evanston. I know they moved to Boston, and I think they had to come back to Chicago for work and- oh no, I remember now! Sorry! So my dad had to come back to Chicago for work, and we lived in a suburb called Geneva— far, far out west. And my other side of grandparents, my mom's parents owned a place by St. Francis Hospital and my parents didn't really have a lot of money to buy a new place, and we didn't really like where we lived, but my grandparents let them rent it out, so when we moved there we got to go to Evanston schools.

The positives of ETHS is that it's very welcoming and open, there's a bunch of different types of people. There's pretty much always gonna be— in a smaller community you might feel different, but in Evanston since there's so many different types of people. . . I feel like you're always going to find someone to relate to in terms of whatever you're interested in. And I think that's a really good thing. But. . . negative, I think Evanston sometimes has one specific point of view on things and if you are to go against that point of view, no matter how wrong you are, it kinda turns into— it doesn't really start a discussion, it just kinda starts shaming that other opinion. They're very firm on what they believe.

My experience within Evanston. . . I love it! It's a unique community, I like how it's kind of a city atmosphere but it's kinda closely knit, you know, in terms of community? I guess mainly I really like the city vibe of it, along with things being kinda laid back. In the suburbs— I mean like you kinda get a suburb feel but can still kinda get that city feel.

I think Evanston has made me feel a lot more comfortable with myself, it's kinda made me feel like I can be who I want to be without really caring what other people thought about me. And people don't really care— I mean like people don't really think negatively on other people in Evanston at all. So I guess that really helped me, I guess, be who I wanna be. I feel like in other places people get caught up just trying to fit in— being something they're not. But in Evanston, you can really just be who you want to be, and thrive in whatever you're doing.

If I could change something in Evanston. . . Evanston pretty great. . . maybe a bowling alley? I mean we talk about diversity a lot, and we talk about it a lot in the beginning of the year, obviously, because of Senior Studies. But it really is very segregated in terms of the neighborhoods that people live in and financial situations. . .

and schools too, so I guess maybe making things more integrated. So students and just people in general can get the experiences and opportunities that other people who are in different places than them can get.

My project— I am working with Connections for the Homeless. First of all, I'm organizing a clothes drive to provide clothes for Connections for the Homeless and second, I'm having a pop up shop for a company I created, called "Merch Vintage". And all the proceeds to that are gonna go to Connections for the Homeless. It being a company that I've made in the past, it's a very specific type of style and its stuff that I've collected through thrift stores and friends who have had that type of clothing. It's like retro, vintage: Ralph Lauren, Tommy Hilfiger, Nautica a bunch of— it's very sports oriented I guess so there's a lot of Olympic stuff. And that stuff I've just kind of thrifted throughout the years, and I've continued to do that, so I have a bunch of clothes that I've collected through that and that's what I'm gonna sell at the pop up shop.

Caroline Springer

I love Evanston with a passion, I was born here and lived in the same house and gone to Evanston public schools for my whole life. I have really loved growing up in Evanston and would love to live here later in life. I definitely have a new outlook on Evanston after taking Senior Studies. Lots of times Evanston's residents praise Evanston for its diversity, and I've definitely done that throughout my whole life. But Senior Studies definitely makes you take a step back, identify its flaws and holds you accountable for changing it. Because we are this rare case of a town where we are diverse both racially and economically, and we are able to identify our issues due to our diversity. I think Evanston residents need to realize this more and not believe we are treating everyone equally just because we are diverse.

So for my project I'm basically doing a career exploration in special education and deaf education, so two to three days of the week I volunteer at Park School in a high school classroom where half of the students have some sort of hearing loss and use American Sign Language. I am not only doing a career exploration I am also trying to create a program between ETHS Students and Park students to help form relationships in the community between people with and without cognitive and physical disabilities. My dream would be to have a group of ETHS students who would be interested in building relationships with students at Park, who could go and work with the kids there.

Living in Evanston has made me more aware of my identity, I am very aware of how being white and being a woman affects my day to day life. This year alone, being the most mature I have ever been, I've become more aware of my white privilege. Just kind of realizing that a voice of a white person is more heard and more respected than a person of color's voice. And learning how to step back and let others be heard, and also knowing when to use your privilege for good. And also, growing up in a place like Evanston, which is very liberal, I have been lucky enough to be surrounded by many strong women and feminists, which has really shaped me— just as a human.

Maggie Stone

My parents were born in Wilmette and then they went to New Trier. And my dad— I think lived in Glencoe for a little. . . maybe he was born in Glencoe I'm not sure. You know, northern suburbs. But then they move to Evanston after living in Chicago for a little bit. And we've lived in the same house for like 20 something years, so I've lived in the same house my whole life.

I have had the opportunity because Evanston is so diverse, to become friends with like many people that look different than me and I think that's great because they're probably going to be some of my lifelong friends and through them I've seen like different cultures and different opinions on different values. And I think that's made me like more open-minded and accepting. I think throughout high school I just cared too much about what people thought of me and I think the whole "popularity thing" was something that was instilled in me in like middle school, like the fact that I paid attention to it, like I even cared about who is popular and who wasn't, and it wasn't until like last year/this year when I was like, "Why the frick do I care about this?" And I think that that just kind of put me down often, like I put myself down often throughout high school.

I love going to public school like I couldn't imagine my life in like a private school, I don't think my parents ever intended to send me to private school. I went to Kingsley and then Haven and then the teachers there were all great. If I remember correctly Kingsley was pretty diverse, but I can't report on like experiences of minorities and stuff like that. But I remember I was on bus two which meant that bus to went to South Evanston and then it came to like my part of Evanston, and so I was always one of the only like, white kids on the bus. But I think that that's where I formed such tight bonds with people who don't look like me. But then some of my friends who are from other parts of North Evanston they took a bus one, which was like all of North Evanston, so. . . But Haven wasn't that diverse I don't think. There was this thing that we read an AP English last year, like, *Why Are All of the Black Kids Sitting Together* or something, I just find that so interesting and so relatable like in school I definitely noticed the fact that— I think elementary school wasn't as much but in middle school you start to form like cliques and groups and stuff and that's when people start to congregate with people that looked like themselves. And that's for sure when I noticed that there was segregation. And in my opinion that segregation within the school hasn't gotten better in the high school.

I for sure would like to see some change and just not like falsely– like in learning our history and stuff, it's so interesting to me and I obviously was oblivious to like that whole thing. But it's important to recognize that like even in a community where everyone thinks that like, "*Evanston is amazing and like so diverse.*" Has its problems with like sugarcoating its history. I also think that it's interesting to see how much like, "*Evanston is diverse*" preached but then if you look at our town it's just like a straight line that like segregates us. And also it's like very liberal which I don't have a problem with but at the same time I think that that creates a lack of conversation like— diversity of conversation. And a lot of people think that like, "*Oh if all my friends in Evanston are with me then the whole world must be with me.*" But that is just not the case, and it's going to be like a reality check for lot of people to realize that there are people who have very different political views in them.

Ever since we watch *The Thirteenth*, I changed my project to do more research on the criminal justice system. Specifically, on the mental and physical affects that prison has on someone, and even more specifically what happens to a drug addict and a person in solitary confinement. And then I'm taking my research and I'm choreographing a dance to show the effects of prison on someone's mind and body. And I just recently started teaching the dance like a group of people who want to be in it and then I'm presenting it at my presentation.

Laura Tataille

Okay so, both my parents were born in Haiti, in this town called Petit Goave— it's very tiny. . . so everyone knows everyone. And then, they came to Evanston— or just America in general, to live a better life. They wanted like, more opportunities and stuff, because obviously Haiti's a third world country and they can't get the opportunities that they would there, here. I don't know why they chose Evanston specifically, but. . . here we are! I know that at first we lived in like Rodgers Park, in like the Chicago area. And I think Evanston because of Evanston Township High School— like they heard really good things about it so. I think I lived in Rogers Park for like a year of my life and then I moved here. So we've been in Evanston for like 17 years.

Positives of Evanston. . . I would say, expanding my friend group, really— like just meeting a lot of new, different people. Negatives. . . I would say being very closed off in like, higher classes, because I am an African American female. I know that in my AP classes I was one of the four black people in that class. And right now I'm only the only black person in my German class, and I remember like, during the beginning of the year, my teacher was like, *"Yeah, like a lot of people think that this is a very white washed language. . ."* and then everyone looked at me, and I was just like, so uncomfortable. But, I feel like that's a negative, like it's very obvious that my skin color plays a role in how I go about my everyday life in high school.

I've talked about my identity a lot in my sociology class, that's literally like all we talked about! I had Mr. Winchester last semester and he really focused on, *"Who are you as a person?"* and like, *"What makes you, you?"* So I think, in finding my identity, it stemmed from being asked that question. You know what I mean? So just like starting that conversation and really like going from there.

As a whole I would say Evanston is pretty good, I mean I've lived here all of my life so I don't have anything to compare it to. I like how it's very diverse (but also very like obviously segregated). I'm pretty sure we've talked about this before, how like you can cross a line and there's a specific type of people there, like they're like a certain color and then you can go to like. . . Howard street area and it's like predominately African American and then you go to like Devon street (which I know is not Evanston) but like it's predominantly Indian and Muslim. But like Evanston I would say, certain parts of it are very diverse, like the area that I live in, there's like a pretty good group of people there, that come from like different backgrounds and stuff.

I would say that recently gentrification has become a big issue. With like Peckish Pig being one of them and like the Starbucks that opened by ETHS. I just don't want Evanston to lose touch with its roots because I know that once we do, that's gonna suck, you know? So I think I want— I don't want people to lose sight of like what Evanston was before, even though we've grown a lot as a city.

I think it would be cool if like people did more research, on like the political side of Evanston, and like the mayors in Evanston and like the city as a whole because a lot— I dunno, a lot of the times we focus on like the higher powers, like the president and stuff who doesn't have like. . . an immediate effect on us but I think it would be cool if like kids in high school focused on who the candidates were— like Devon Reid or like stuff like that. You know? If they like really went up on that and like knew who would like be making immediate change, if that makes any sense. I dunno, cause I'm like ignorant to that, so if a lot of people read up on that stuff then there'd be a lot more change.

So for my project, I'm working with the homeless people in Evanston and Chicago and then ultimately I'm comparing the two. So for my essential question, I'm having three questions within one: "*What is homelessness*? *Why is it caused*? *What are the solutions to homelessness*?" And so within that I'm raising funds for Connections for the Homeless, because that's where I work two days of the week. And then I'm also involved in an art contest where people can submit entries to have posters hung up around Evanston. . . and like yard signs and also just like coffee shops or anything like that, and then I'm also doing a benefit concert in April. There's artists from ETHS that are performing, tickets are 5 dollars and then all of the proceeds are going to Connections for the Homeless.

Ruby Tortuga

Both of my parents were born in Chicago actually, and we ended up in Evanston for the schools.

Some positive experiences here were that I've had some great teachers and also just like meeting great people, and just like really interesting classes. Some negative experiences here has just been like the segregation of the school. And like how certain classes will have mostly white people and how certain classes might not be like that. And that's kind of like by class and like by— how if you're in an AP class then you're probably going to be white. So like thats one of the disadvantages that you see in the school. Last year I took one AP class, which was English and I kind of hated it because like everyone was white so I just felt like– also everyone have the same viewpoint and everyone was just reiterating what everyone said so it's kind of. . . just really boring. And at the same time I was in US history, I was just in a mixed honors class and it was really interesting, there were a lot of different viewpoints, it was all different races and just such a different dynamic, and I thought that was really interesting to see back to back.

I mean I haven't lived in Evanston my whole life. I lived in Mount Carrol which is like this really small town in southern Illinois for a few years, and I really loved it there. But I was like six so it was nice that I was in a small town but I think I would've hated it there now, so I'm glad I got out of there. And then I also lived in Chicago with my mom for like six years and that overlapped with when my dad got a place in Evanston. And I remember at the Chicago school I went to, my teacher was really mean, I only went to one Chicago school for one year. And my teacher– I remember one time she wouldn't let this kid go to the bathroom and like told him to pee his pants. And he did. So it's like, that experience would not happen here. Like that teacher would've gotten fired. So at that time, to me, that was just okay and I didn't even see anything wrong with it, it just kind of stuck with me. And now I see that like a second grader should just be allowed to go to the bathroom. But I think at the Evanston schools the teachers are better.

In middle school it was really weird because the teachers were like really racist in a lot of ways. I went to Nichols and the teachers would just say things like– well like one thing was the Constitution Test. Like there was this packet that you'd get and it had all of the answers on it basically and the white kids basically had to fill out the packet, while any person of color got the packet already filled in. And it was just like assuming that if you are a person of color you are not as smart. . . and that was kind of the way that the classes were set up in general as well, like the people of color got the extra help because it was assumed that they weren't as smart or something.

ANNIE: Sorry to interrupt quickly but you were in Jedi? Right? (Like the different teams, like your class section) and I noticed that like, I feel like a lot of Latino kids were in Jedi.

RUBY: Yeah, Jedi was like the "bilingual" one. That's where all of the Latino kids were and there were some white people.

ANNIE: I feel like all of those Latino kids– like they all spoke English perfectly, like they could've been in any class.

RUBY: Yeah I remember there was only one person who didn't speak perfect English, but he had English he just wasn't completely fluent, and that was it.

ANNIE: I always thought that was so strange.

RUBY: Yeah, really weird! It didn't make any sense at all, it was just really weird that they would just group everyone. I wouldn't be surprised if I was there because my last name is Tortuga *laughs* like that wouldn't have been a surprise to me. But yeah that was a weird experience, I thought middle school was a really weird experience. And high school kind of toned down from that but you still see a lot of that, it's just not as obvious.

So like what I was talking about with AP classes and like how you're put on a track, and even though tracking isn't as much of a thing anymore it's still there, and you're put on this track at a very young age whether you're in like the higher math in like elementary and middle school— or like if you're asked onto that math team, and there are certain people that were asked on and certain people that weren't. I don't know so there's just like that inequality at schools. I don't know also like working at a restaurant, I saw like people will expect me to be prettier when I was a hostess they'd be like, "*Oh you need to put that beautiful smile on your face.*" and things like that. And then working in the back of the house people– they're just so sexist. And so– well they would talk to me, like the sous chef would like constantly be talking to me about how he wants to (he's 26, he was married) how he wants to be my boyfriend. . . and he loves me, and how beautiful I am.. . . And this is when I'm in the kitchen, I'm wearing my chef uniform, and it's like why would that be a topic of conversation ever? And so those are some things that I've seen.

My project is on food waste and redistribution. So I've been going to different grocery stores and either asking for donations or going behind and digging through their dumpsters and taking whatever food there is. And so I've hosted a benefit dinner where the proceeds went to DREAMERS club and I'm hosting another one in May and right now I'm only eating food waste for a month. It's all edible food waste so I'll go dumpster diving almost every single day and I get donations from different places. I have so much food, I'm feeding my family most nights too because I just have too much food! We waste like 40% of the food!

www.ingramcontent.com/pod-product-compliance
Lightning Source LLC
Chambersburg PA
CBHW031601110426
42742CB00036B/644